ALONE ON THE SOUTH DOWNS WAY

A TALE OF TWO JOURNEYS FROM WINCHESTER TO EASTBOURNE

HOLLY WORTON

Alone on the South Downs Way:
A Tale of Two Journeys from Winchester to Eastbourne

Holly Worton

Tribal Publishing Ltd

First published in 2016
Published in this edition 2020

ISBN 978-1-911161-40-0 EPUB
ISBN 978-1-911161-41-7 MOBI
ISBN 978-1-911161-42-4 Paperback

A CIP catalogue record for this book is available from the British Library

"The Downs... too much for one pair of eyes, enough to float a whole population in happiness, if only they would look."

— VIRGINIA WOOLF, *DIARIES*

DISCLAIMER

Although the author and publisher have made every effort to ensure that the information in this book was correct at press time, the author and publisher do not assume and hereby disclaim any liability to any party for any loss, damage, or disruption caused by errors or omissions, whether such errors or omissions result from negligence, accident, or any other cause.

The information in this book is meant to supplement, not replace, proper walking and hiking training and planning with a guidebook. Like any sport involving physical exertion, equipment, balance, and environmental factors, long distance walking poses some inherent risk. The author and publisher advise readers to take full responsibility for their safety and to know their own personal limits. Before practicing the skills described in this book, be sure that your equipment is well maintained, and do not take risks beyond your level of experience, aptitude, training, and comfort level.

Personal responsibility is important. Ultimately, only you are responsible for your own safety. Please keep this in mind, especially when walking alone. And...be sure to enjoy your journey!

CONTENTS

SOUTH DOWNS
WAY

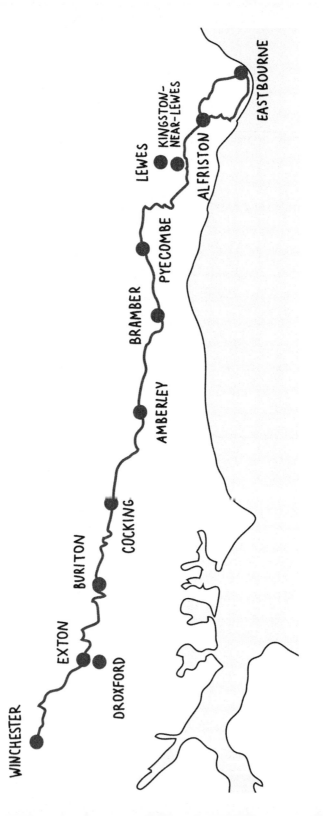

PREFACE

It's the year 2020 when I write this, almost five years after I first walked the South Downs Way in 2015. I've learned a lot since my first long-distance walking adventure: I've walked another National Trail—the Ridgeway—I've walked shorter routes like the Downs Link and the Wey-South Path, and I've walked the Camino Portugues. Each time I was able to refine my training, my preparation, and my process of walking a long-distance trail.

I'm very much aware that the first edition of this book may have been a bit off-putting to some people. I had a rough time of it, and the walk was much more challenging than I anticipated. There were a lot of blisters, sweat, and tears. It certainly didn't paint my experience as an inspiring one. But it was the reality of my adventure.

That's why I was so anxious to re-walk the South Downs Way a second time in 2019 and apply all that I had learned in the previous four years. I was curious as to what it would be like—was I an absolute disaster as a long-distance walker, or could it be easier? (Spoiler alert: it was very, very different the second time around, which is why I've gone ahead with this second edition of the book.)

If you want to read a lovely account of walking the South Downs Way, full of energy, wonder, and joy—then read Part III of this book, titled The Pleasure. If you want all the blisters, sweat, and tears of my first adventure—then read Part I, appropriately titled The Pain. It's up to you how you read this book, of course. My point is that you may not necessarily want to read my story in chronological order. You might want to avoid Part I altogether!

However you choose to approach this book, I hope that you learn something from my experience. I've been careful to share my mistakes so that you can avoid making them yourself. The South Downs Way is a magical adventure, and I hope you find it to be every bit as joyful as I did...the second time around.

Holly Worton
April 2020

PART I

THE PAIN

INTRODUCTION

Walking, for me, is a spiritual activity. It's about so much more than just getting exercise, or seeing new things. I have always felt a strong connection to Nature (yes, I capitalize Nature—it's that important to me), and this has increased in recent years, with my enrollment in the Order of Bards, Ovates and Druids where I have worked through their Bardic course and now their Ovate course. I have deepened my spiritual connection to Nature even more through the Shamanic Plant Spirit Healing Apprenticeship that I graduated from in 2019.

But it was walking in the outdoors that first helped me to strengthen my relationship with Nature. And as a result, I have found that the more long Nature walks I take, the more I deepen the connection with myself. Long walks in Nature help me to disconnect from thoughts and worries and enter into a state of what I call mobile meditation in the outdoors. That's the best way I can describe it. I put one foot in front of the other, and my mind quiets.

I've loved walking outdoors for years, and yet sometimes it feels like walking is a new interest of mine. I've been walking a lot more since I moved to England, and in particular, since I moved to the area where I currently live, a small town just off the North Downs Way within the Surrey Hills Area of Outstanding Natural Beauty. There are so many lush green footpaths to explore, and it's become an increasing passion of mine.

But my interest in walking and hiking began back when I was a teenager. I grew up in California in a small town called Clayton, in a house located just down the street from the Mt. Diablo State Park. It was no more than ten minutes on foot from my house, which meant that I spent many scorching hot summer afternoons exploring the trails with my friends, who were surprisingly willing to be dragged up the mountain by me.

Mt. Diablo has that same gorgeous golden beauty of the surrounding hills of the San Francisco Bay Area: it's blanketed with dry yellow grasses and low growing manzanita shrubs. I often think that the reason that I love where I live now so much is that it resembles a lush green version of the area I grew up in, sans mountain. The Surrey Hills Area of Outstanding Natural Beauty is filled with rolling green hills as far as the eye can see, with little towns and villages nestled into the valleys.

Sadly, when I went to university, my passion for hiking and exploring waned, which was especially unfortunate, considering that the hills surrounding San Luis Obispo were filled with gorgeous places to walk. I was in the middle of a period of my life where I became profoundly disconnected from who I really was and what I loved deep down, and it's taken me many years to reconnect with myself since then.

From there, I moved to Spain, then Los Angeles, Mexico, and Argentina, where I all but abandoned my love for hiking. Despite being surrounded by lush jungle where I lived in southeast Mexico, it was only in Chile—where my company owned property and was setting up a new project—that I rekindled my love for hiking. There, I spent some time exploring Patagonia on foot and horseback.

Eventually, I ended up in England, where I was inspired to revive my deep passion for walking in Nature. It all started one day when I was in a bookstore. I had browsed through the stacks and was on my way out when a book caught my eye: *Time Out Country Walks Vol. 1: 50 Walks Near London.* I walked straight to it, briefly leafed through the pages, and went directly to the till to purchase it.

That summer, for my birthday in July, I set off on my first walk from the book: walk number 29, from Hassocks to Lewes, which interestingly follows part of the South Downs Way for the middle portion of the journey. This birthday walk was my first experience with the South Downs Way. Since then, I've walked over fifteen of the routes detailed in that guidebook, and I've spent hours and hours exploring new paths on my own.

Perhaps sparked by my love for day hikes, I've been fascinated with the idea of doing a long-distance walk. For twenty years, I've wanted to walk the Camino de Santiago. And finally, in 2015, I booked the dates in my calendar for April 2016. About the time that I committed to walking the Camino, I spent weeks reading everything I could about it. I read both practical guides and websites and also walking journals, the more in-depth stories of people's inner journeys as they walked the Way of St. James.

It seemed that so many of the people who decided to walk the Camino had never completed a long-distance trail on their own—and at that point, neither had I. Though I was an avid walker, not batting an eye at embarking on a five- or six-hour weekend walk in the woods, I had never actually walked several days in a row. I was perfectly fine with one or two long walks on the weekend, but I'd never gone beyond that.

Why the South Downs Way

And that's why I decided to walk the South Downs Way, a National Trail that stretches 100 miles (160 km.) between Winchester in the west and Eastbourne in the east...or the other way around, depending on how you walk it. The Way runs entirely within the South Downs National Park, located in the Southeast of England, with easy access from the greater London area.

The trail stretches across the counties of Hampshire, West Sussex, and East Sussex, and it's dotted with villages and small towns throughout, which means that it's easy to find places to stay, whether you're looking for B&Bs or inns. Youth hostels and campgrounds are a bit harder to find, but there are some along the Way if you want to make your journey a little more economical. It's also one of just two National Trails that can be used along its full length by cyclists and horse riders in addition to walkers.

The trail runs along a chalk ridge along the top of the Downs, which means that it drains and dries out quickly, keeping the path reasonably dry even when it's been raining. In England, downs are rounded, grass-covered hills that are typically composed of chalk. The name derives from the Old English word dūn, which means "hill". The elevated position of the Way provides excellent views of the surrounding hills and valleys, even as far south as the coast and the Isle of Wight, which sits just offshore.

The Way, when walked from west to east, winds up and down through woodland, then fields of wheat, barley, and oats, pastures full of sheep and cows, and finally across the open chalk cliffs of the Seven Sisters. The woods, fields, and cliffs make for great variety in terms of scenery, which is essential for me in a pleasant walk.

How I planned my walk

In preparing my journey, I consulted several websites, including blogs and the National Trails website (you can find specific details in the Resources section at the end of this book). Most people plan to walk the South Downs Way in either seven, eight, or nine days, so I decided to go with eight, which seemed like a medium pace. I didn't want to rush, and eight days felt like a reasonable length of time: I'd depart on a Saturday and return on a Saturday, which would leave me one day to recover physically on Sunday before getting back into normal life.

The other consideration was whether to walk it from west to east (Winchester to Eastbourne), or the other way around. It felt logical to end my journey by the sea with a spectacular view, rather than inland at a cathedral (my adventure could be described as a spiritual pilgrimage, but it was a Nature pilgrimage, not a religious one), so I decided to walk from Winchester to Eastbourne. The final day of walking toward Eastbourne was known for its incredible views. Plus, if you walk from west to east, the wind will be behind you rather than in your face, which never makes for easy walking.

The South Downs Way is considered an "easy" walk in terms of difficulty. However, there are a lot of ups and downs as the trail winds its way through woodland, farmland, and finally, the rolling hills of the Seven Sisters on the coast. Most days start with an uphill hike to the top of the ridge, and end with a downhill slope toward the village where you'll be staying, with several ups and downs in between. It's best to have some walking or hiking experience before you start on this journey, especially in a hilly environment.

What to expect from this book

Before I continue, I need to clarify that this book is not a guide-book. It's intended to be a walking journal: the story of one person's experience of walking the South Downs Way (twice)... with some added information at the end that you may find useful in planning your walk. This journey will be different for everyone who completes it, and as you'll be able to see from my two adventures, it can be very, very different each time the same person walks the same trail.

I enjoy reading blogs and books about other people's walking journeys. In addition to the guidebook I used to prepare for this trip (the Trailblazer Publications guide), I found Martin King's *The Irreverent Guide to Walking and Cycling the South Downs Way* to be both useful and entertaining. It helped me get inspired to do the walk in a way that the guide-book didn't. King's book is the only book that relates a personal account of walking (and cycling) the Way that I could find, and I wanted to contribute my own story to the offerings.

In telling my story, I hope to inspire you to embark on a solo long-distance walk of your own, whether it's on the South Downs Way or somewhere else. If you're terrified at the thought of walking alone for eight days, then I ask you to open your mind to the possibility. I hear from a lot of women who really question whether or not it's safe to do a walk like this by themselves. I think it is. And if you've got any kind of beliefs or fears that might be preventing you from planning a walk of this Nature, I invite you to set those aside for the moment. Listen to my story, and please consider the possibility for yourself.

For now, let's start on our journey along the South Downs Way. Come with me and discover what it's like to walk from Winchester to Eastbourne in what must have been the hottest, sunniest week of the year. I invite you to walk along with me as the South Downs Way opens up before us, down woodland paths and between fields of wheat, oats, and barley. We'll explore ancient historical sites dating back to the Roman occupation of England and even as far back as the Bronze Age. This is a journey back in time as much as it is a journey in Nature.

Each chapter reflects a day on my walk, and is divided into three sections: morning, walk, and evening. I wrote much of this book on my iPad as I traveled along the Way—while waiting for my dinner in the evenings or before heading down for breakfast in the mornings—and I added additional information during the months after my return.

Despite my initial enthusiasm for publishing this book as soon as possible after finishing the Way, I found that revisiting the book every couple of months to add my reflections on the journey rounded out my description of the experience. At the time of the last round of editing of the first edition of this book, it had been almost a year since my journey, giving me plenty of time and distance to reflect on everything that happened. Now, as I'm putting together the second edition, it's been almost five years since I walked the South Downs Way. I've learned a lot since then. To me, this makes for a much richer account of my walk.

I was never lonely on the Way, but I certainly was alone for long periods. There were walkers whom I crossed paths with every day, and there were cyclists and runners who whizzed past me every once in a while, but I was mostly alone on my walk along the South Downs Way. This pleasant solitude gave me a sense of absolute freedom and a deep connection to the surrounding Nature.

Daily themes

I am a massive fan of oracle cards, and before going to bed the night before I departed for my South Downs Way journey, I pulled eight cards from Lisa McLoughlin's Plant Ally card deck.

Oracle cards are a deck of cards with different images and themes on them, and are used to gain a sense of insight, perspective, clarity, and inspiration. They can also be used for divination. Essentially, you set your intention or ask your question as you shuffle the cards, and then you lay them out face down and select one or more cards to answer your question or give you guidance on the situation at hand. I love drawing cards for specific occasions: each October and November, when I do my annual planning and goal setting for the following year, I pull one card for each month of the year. It gets me excited about what's to come in each month, and the predictions are amazingly accurate.

I thought it would be fun to pull a card for each day of my walk, both to give me an idea of what might lay ahead for me and also give me something to focus on each day of my journey. I would later learn just how important this small detail would be in helping me get through every day. It's something that I started with this South Downs Way walk and continued to do for later long-distance trails.

This was as much an inner journey as it was a walking journey, and I'm very candid about my experience: you'll get both the inner and the outer bits in this book. As I said, long-distance walking gets me into a state of mobile meditation. Walking the South Downs Way was one of the most satisfying and magical experiences of my life, despite (or perhaps because of?) the unexpected challenges that presented themselves along the way. The end came all too soon, and I was tempted to savor the final bits of my walk at a snail's pace, with more frequent stops than on previous days. It was like approaching the end of a good book: I didn't want the experience to be over.

I hope you enjoy the experience as much as I did, and I hope the challenging bits don't put you off doing your long-distance walk. I promise you; it doesn't need to be as tricky as it was for me this first time. Let's get started.

DAY 1

The card for Day 1 was Wild Rose—Pure Joy. You can probably imagine from what you've read so far that I wasn't yet feeling much joy, but I hoped things would change as soon as I got out in Nature and on the Way. There's something magical and exciting about starting on a new walk, and I was hoping to feel that soon.

The Morning

I began writing this book on my iPad on the train to Winchester, the city where I started my South Downs walk. I had started planning this trip less than three months prior, and now that it had finally started, I almost couldn't believe it was happening. On our walk to the rail station, my husband Agustín kept asking me how I was feeling. Honestly? I had no idea. It felt very abstract. It was like it wasn't happening.

I didn't have that giddy excitement I usually got when setting out on a new day walk, which, to be honest, was a bit confusing. I loved new walks: exploring new territory by following a predetermined route, or by using a map, or even just setting out on a new trail, with no idea of where it would take me. It's exciting. It feels adventurous. It's like Christmas in the woods, with new gifts appearing before me in the form of visual delights.

But I wasn't getting that feeling this morning. Perhaps I was taking the walk too seriously. Maybe my expectations were too high. It had been *the* topic of discussion ever since I made the decision to walk one hundred miles along the South Downs. I had told everyone I knew, whenever I could work it into the conversation. Perhaps it was my way of getting accountability, of making sure it would happen. If everyone knew about it, then I couldn't back out of actually doing it.

I had all the gear: great boots, a great backpack, and everything else I needed for an eight-day walk. I had the niggling feeling, however, that I might have a bit too much gear: my friend Adam Wells, a Camino de Santiago transformational coach based in London, recommends that you pack no more than 10% of your body weight, or at most 8kg. My backpack weighed in at 9kg, including the day's lunch, snacks, and water. That was more than 10% of my body weight.

I'd be lying if I said I hadn't felt concerned about walking with that much weight on my back. I had kept my packing list to the minimum and had continued to pare things down at the last minute, swapping my standard wallet for a much smaller, lighter one. I had pulled the essentials from the main one: cash and just three cards. Unfortunately, in my zeal to reduce weight in my bag, I had left my railcard at home, which meant having to pay full price for my train ticket.

This error annoyed me to no end, and it felt like an ominous start to the journey. I hate making mistakes. I hate being sloppy. My mind gremlins use it as an excuse to beat myself up internally. And thus, my first lesson of the South Downs Way had been learned: think twice before making last-minute packing changes, and pay attention to what you decide to change. Always plan, and double-check everything. Once you've left home, there are some things you can pick up on the way, and some things that you can't. A railcard is one of those. However, it was hardly a tragic error, and I chalked it up as a mental note to pay more attention in the future. I do try to learn from my mistakes.

In the end, I decided to set off from home with this overweight pack, rather than reducing the load even more. I had a long list of walks planned for the future, and some of them involved camping, which meant that I'd need to bring a tent, a sleeping bag, and food in addition to everything I had already packed. That would make for an even more massive pack (for backpacking, some recommend a maximum pack weight of 20-30% of your body weight), and I was curious as to whether I would be able to handle a bigger pack on those journeys. I decided to risk the heavier pack on this trip as an experiment for the future.

I planned to report back at the end of the walk on any unnecessary items that I took—things that weighed my bag down unnecessarily (I include a list of these things in the appendix at the end of this book). I can tell you, however, that from Day 1, I was already very aware of one such item: my iPad 2 and the keyboard that I was using to write. I had debated long and hard about whether to bring the iPad or a paper journal or a notebook, but the iPad won out in the end: it made writing faster and more comfortable, and it doubled as a book (multiple books, even). I had loaded up three new Kindle books for this walk so that I could read in the evening before bed. Still, I was very aware of the extra weight that it added to my pack.

Now, in retrospect, I find it hilarious that I was so fixated on the extra weight that the iPad added to my pack when in reality, the problem was the excess weight I had been carrying on my body. I have an under-active thyroid, and I had gained weight a few years before this walk, and the fact was that it made everything a little more complicated. This is not to say that you shouldn't embark on a long-distance walk if you're overweight, but it is something to be aware of. I now understand this, but at the time, it was easier to blame everything on the iPad.

The Walk

My first day's walk began at Winchester Cathedral. The trail passed through the village of Chilcomb, then Cheesefoot Head and Beacon Hill, before finishing in Exton, the smallest of the little villages located in the Meon valley. From there, I had another two miles to walk to my accommodation in Droxford. This first stage of the Way starts in a city, but as soon as it leaves Winchester, it is relatively remote, with just one pub along the way for drinks and meals. If you're a snacker, or if you plan to have lunch along the trail, you'll want to stock up on food before you leave Winchester.

It was a quick ten-minute walk from the Winchester train station to Winchester Cathedral, where I started on the official trail. The start of the South Downs Way has since changed, but in 2015 it still began at the cathedral. One of the largest cathedrals in England, it was founded in the year 642 on a site located just to the north of the present construction, which was consecrated in the year 1093. The style is Norman and Gothic. Winchester Cathedral is open every day of the year. Visitor opening times for the cathedral, the crypt, and treasury are from 9:45 am to 5 pm Monday through Saturday and 12:30 to 2:30 pm on Sundays. The admission fee for adults is £9.50. The schedules and pricing are, of course, all subject to change, so if you want to visit the cathedral, please double-check the website before you travel. These times and fees are accurate as of 2020, but both have changed since 2015.

I briefly considered entering the cathedral for a quick visit, but the grounds were full of people, and I imagined there would be just as many inside. I wasn't in the mood for crowds. Plus, I was anxious to start on the trail: I was here to walk in Nature, not to visit historical and religious sites. And so I turned my back on the cathedral and headed toward the South Downs. From the cathedral, it was (in theory) just a matter of following the map in my guidebook and also the signs for the South Downs Way. I hadn't brought any additional maps aside from my guidebook, as everything I had read about the South Downs Way led me to believe that it was well signposted all along the trail.

And it was very well signposted—except for the way out of Winchester. I only got lost once during this first day's walk: just out of Winchester, before I entered the countryside. It's well known that navigation for many long-distance trails is more difficult in urban areas than it is in rural ones, and Winchester is no exception. I walked uphill along a quiet, shady road through a residential area. At one point, I stopped, checked my guidebook, and adjusted my route. I had been walking on a road that was roughly parallel to the one I was supposed to be on.

I ended up following what appeared to be the official route until I crossed the A3 (a major road connecting London and Portsmouth) and then couldn't figure out where to go on the other side. I wandered around for a couple of minutes, searching for a sign that would indicate which way to head, but there was none to be found. That was my first indication that I was off course yet again. It was not a great start to my 100-mile walk, and with the roar of traffic on the road below me, I was getting frustrated. I was now desperate to get out of the city and into Nature.

It turned out I had used the wrong bridge to cross the road: the one I had crossed was a wide bridge, for both cars and foot traffic. Fortunately, I was still in an urban environment and had a 4G connection on my mobile. Google Maps pointed me in the right direction: a smaller bridge just for pedestrians a bit farther down and only a ten minute walk away, down a leafy green path that ran parallel to the noisy A3. I could see the bridge from where I was located, which made it even easier to access the correct one. I backtracked my steps across the first bridge and headed down the right path, accompanied by the roar of the traffic on the busy road to my left. I couldn't wait to get away from the bustle of civilization and into the peace of the woods.

I was also very frustrated with myself: remember what I said about how much I hate to make mistakes? It seemed like this first day of my walk was going to wake up all of my mind gremlins and get them babbling inside my head. I always feel like I've wasted time when I get lost on a walk, and I give myself a hard time about it. I don't just think that I've spent time, but that I've also wasted energy. It's as though I set up my mind to walk a certain distance, and when I get lost and go out of my way, it annoys me that I've added more miles to my journey. God forbid I should stray from the original plan. Sometimes, I'm terrible about being flexible.

Yet life is so often like this: we have a set path that we've decided on, and sometimes we get lost along the way. We may also consciously stray from our path: sometimes we make new decisions and we pivot off the path that we've been on and move to a different one. That may, of course, add extra time to the journey. But it's all part of life. Things aren't always a direct path from A to B. Often the path squiggles all around before we arrive at our intended destination. At a rational level, I honestly don't believe that our journey or our path in life is *meant* to be a straight, direct one. These detours, where we either get lost or purposely stray from our path, can be enriching. Often they're the bits where we learn the most. It can be frustrating, but we often learn valuable lessons in the process. At an emotional level, however, I often wish that life was a straight path.

Speaking of lessons: there is, of course, another way of looking at this: each time I get lost on the trail, it's a reminder to pay attention—to be alert—so that I can stay on the correct path. Paying attention is essential in the outdoors, and it's necessary for life: if we don't keep our eye on our intended route, we won't reach our destination. The lesson I could have learned here (and didn't) was to pay more attention to the maps and signs on the Way. Unfortunately, this was something that I wouldn't learn until the second day of my walk, when I got lost yet again, adding a much longer detour to my journey. I like to think that I learn from my mistakes, but sometimes it takes making them multiple times before it finally sinks in. There are times when I'm a fast learner, and there are times when—it takes me a while.

Despite knowing on a rational level that getting lost can be such a great learning experience—and that it can lead to discoveries—I still find it frustrating to embark on these unintended detours when I'm walking. I reflected on this as I headed off on the actual South Downs Way. Flexibility has never been a strong point for me, though I had certainly improved in this area over recent years. My thinking could be rigid sometimes.

It had become easier for me to accept changes in life, but it was still a challenge at times. The difficulty is probably a result of my autistic brain, which wants to have everything perfectly planned out well in advance, and then it wants things to go exactly to plan. It doesn't do well with unexpected changes. The South Downs, however, were about to teach me many lessons about things not going to plan.

I followed the signs down and around the urban pathway until it crossed through a kissing gate (this is a small gate which is hung within a U- or V-shaped enclosure and lets just one person through at a time) and into the countryside. It was like a magical gateway that separated urban Winchester from the pure Nature of the South Downs. The second I passed through the gate, I saw a deer dart off into the woods. Was this a sign of some sort? I rarely saw deer when I was out walking, and I was pleasantly surprised to see one so close to the city. It felt like the perfect welcome to the long journey ahead of me, almost as if Nature were saying hello—and then immediately running away. But that's what deer do, so nothing was surprising or ominous about that.

I paused to pull out my water bottle and have a drink. The day was hot and sunny, with clear blue skies, and I was already thirsty. I needed to remind myself to keep hydrated, as I wasn't used to such warm weather on my walks. This was, after all, England: land of crisp gray skies, which make for perfect walking weather. I had planned my walk for the last week of June and the beginning of July because I had hoped the weather would be reasonably decent then. I could never have imagined just how hot and sunny these eight days would be, making the Way even more challenging than it might have been otherwise. It was hot from the very start of the journey, and it would continue to be so throughout the week, rising to record temperatures.

After returning the bottle to my pack, I pulled my walking poles from their bag and twisted them together. I usually avoid using poles when walking in an urban environment because they're not necessary and can be noisy and annoying, but now that I was on an actual dirt trail, it was time to get them ready. I use Pacerpoles, a different kind of walking poles that help me keep my rhythm when walking, assist in maintaining good posture, and essentially turn me into what the Pacerpole creators call a "double biped." Most importantly, they help keep me on my feet. I can be incredibly clumsy when walking— hello autism—sometimes hilariously slipping and sliding down the trails. I've never injured myself on a walk, but I can be ridiculously bumbling on my feet. Pacerpoles help me prevent disastrous falls.

It usually takes me some time to get into the rhythm of a walk: that beautiful state of quiet mobile meditation in Nature. Sometimes it can take me as much as two or three hours to get into the flow. But the start of this walk was full of minor irritations that further awakened my mind gremlins and delayed my meditative process. Rather than enjoying the pure beauty of Nature, I was caught up in a series of minor annoyances.

First, it was the cyclists. At the start of the walk, two signs indicated where cyclists were meant to go. This signage appeared on various stages of the South Downs Way: sometimes, the trail would split into a footpath and a bridleway, which is what the cyclists were meant to follow. The path that I was on at the start of the journey was a footpath, marked for walkers only.

And yet there were cyclists headed every which way, which annoyed me to no end because I usually don't hear them until they're just behind me, at which point I practically jump out of my shoes in shock when their tires crunch through the leaves on the trail. I am eternally grateful for cyclists who have a bell and *use it* to let walkers know they're coming. Unfortunately, that was not the case with most of the cyclists I came across on this first morning. My irritation and lack of patience radiated off me like electricity as I speed-walked down the narrow footpath. I was ridiculously annoyed at something as simple as this. I was out in Nature: I should have been enjoying myself! Instead, the trail was triggering all of my mind crap.

The second annoyance (yes, this was multi-layered) was the couple walking ahead of me, who had passed me just after I had gone through the kissing gate into the countryside where I stopped to put my poles together. I have a thing about walking alone: if I'm out alone, then I want to be alone, with no one in my sight, either in front of me or behind. This is one of those silly quirks that I have when I'm walking, and it comes up all the time. I will go great lengths to speed walk and pass someone, so I don't have to look at them on the trail ahead of me. Is this silly? Of course, it is. And thankfully, this is something that no longer bothers me: I do prefer to be alone on a trail, but I'm not so sensitive about seeing other people.

However, on this day—the first of my South Downs adventure, as I clicked with my poles toward the little village of Chilcomb—all I wanted was to be alone in Nature, and I was worried that there would be people everywhere along the entire length of the Way. It is, after all, one of the most easily accessible National Trails, and probably the best known of them. Little did I realize at the time (though now it seems evident to me) that the busiest points were the two ends of the South Downs Way: near Winchester and Eastbourne. I was also starting this walk on the weekend, when there are more people out on the trail. These urban areas have easy access to the Way, and they're popular with both day walkers and weekend walkers. I didn't know this at the time, but once I got into the heart of the South Downs, I would often go for hours without seeing another person. But I hadn't reached that part yet, and I was craving solitude.

When I realized that this couple and I were walking more or less at the same pace, I was even more annoyed. At times I would stop, and they would pass me. Then they'd stop, and I would pass them. We kept trading places on the trail, and I would get annoyed each time it happened. All my usual walking frustrations were bubbling up on this first day of my walk, to eventually be released. From the second day on, I felt much more comfortable going and relaxed as I journeyed down the Way—either that or I had discovered bigger things to worry about on the trail. But on this first day, I was a barrel of irritations. It's fascinating how a bit of alone time can trigger all of our inner troubles and bring them to the surface for us to look at. And when we're mostly alone on a trail, we have no choice but to look at them.

I soon arrived at the little village of Chilcomb, home to the Church of St Andrew, a Grade I listed building that's located less than 10 minutes off the trail. The little Norman church dates back to around 1120-1140. I paused to read a sign that indicated how to find the church and then continued on my journey down the South Downs Way. This would not be a morning for visiting churches. I wanted to continue on my way.

As the trail exited Chilcomb, it wound up and around through farmland. As I walked alongside golden fields of grain, the day grew even hotter, with the sun blazing in the clear blue sky. There was not a cloud in the sky, and there were very few trees in sight. The trail was wide open and unprotected from the shade. It hardly felt like I was in England. It was more like a typical hot, sunny day in California, and it reminded me of hiking when I was in high school. I saw the couple stop to reapply sunscreen, and I realized I hadn't bothered to put any on yet that morning. I found the tube, which I had conveniently placed in the waist strap of my pack, and slathered the cream all over my arms and hands, face, and neck.

The trail curved up and around Telegraph Hill, which had tumuli dotted here and there to the right of the path. I was grateful for my broad-brimmed sun hat, as I am very sensitive to sunshine on my head. It can leave me with a headache by the evening, and even make me feel sick to my stomach. I was sweating profusely by now, and I would soon learn that sunscreen needed to be reapplied regularly in this heat. Day 1 was already proving to be very, very different from my usual weekend day walks.

Many rolling fields and a couple of hours later, I came across two women and a man walking together, and I quickly passed them, which made me feel pleased. Things were looking up! Shortly after, I stopped for lunch, contemplating my fervent desire to be alone on the trail as I munched on my sandwich. As I was pondering my irritation with the presence of others, I became acutely aware of the fact that I was having a leisurely lunch, and that the people would inevitably catch up with me and then pass me once again. I paused to consider an appropriate strategy.

They seemed to be pretty far behind, as they hadn't appeared yet. Either that, or they had taken another route, one of the numerous footpaths or bridleways that branched off the South Downs Way. It was impossible to tell who was just out on a day walk and who was walking the Way without striking up a conversation with the other walkers, and as you can imagine, I wasn't one for conversation when I was out on a walk. I was becoming increasingly aware of just how antisocial I was on the trail. On the one hand, I was happy that I had passed them, so I didn't have them in my view ahead of me, but this, of course, made bathroom stops difficult: I was never sure how much privacy I had before someone would come up behind me on the trail. It felt like a lose-lose situation.

So far, there weren't many big shrubs to hide behind, and I had to be quick about any pit stops. This was an ever-increasing challenge on the South Downs, especially once I got out of Hampshire and into the open farmland of Sussex. It eventually got to the point where there was nowhere to go but in the middle of the trail, and I would nervously turn my head from left to right as I searched for cyclists and walkers that might be coming from one way or the other. Luckily, there were so few people on the Way—once I got away from Winchester— that no one ever surprised me. I've heard of friends coming across people unabashedly having a professional toilet break (think: number two) in the middle of a trail, and I didn't want to become the subject of someone's awkward South Downs Way story.

As I sat there, enjoying my lunch and contemplating my deep desire to walk alone without people in my sight, they passed me. This annoyed me even more because I knew they'd end up walking in front of me once again. I finished my lunch and got up to continue on my walk, and shortly after, I was pleased to pass them as they stopped for lunch alongside the trail. Eventually, they disappeared altogether, and I was alone for the rest of my day's journey—just how I liked it.

Why am I sharing all of my irritations with you? Because on a long-distance trail, the inner journey is as important as the outer journey. The alone time brings up our mind crap—and we can either choose to look at it and work through it, or we can ignore it completely. I was aware of what was coming up for me, but I clearly wasn't ready, able, or willing to actually deal with it at the time. I can only say that I'm very happy that it's since dissipated for me. I'm no longer a frazzled ball of nerves on my walks.

The sun was out with a vengeance. As I mentioned earlier, I had intentionally planned this walk for a time of the year when it's generally lovely out, but it's so tricky to predict British weather. This day was a proper summer: clear blue skies, sun all day long, and hot, hot, hot. I had already applied sunscreen twice on my arms, face, and neck. But despite this, the tops of my hands and lower arms glowed a bright red. This is one thing to remember about walking with poles: your arms and hands are exposed in a way that they aren't when you're walking normally, with your arms at your sides. You need to apply extra sunscreen to prevent burns.

In the heat, I drank through most of my water. I stopped at the only pub on that portion of the trail for a bottle of sparkling water, which I enjoyed in their garden. I plopped myself down on one of the garden tables, and put my feet up. The backpack was already taking its toll on my body. Despite my quick start to the day, I was now walking much slower than usual, and I had so little energy, it sometimes felt like I was trudging along the trail. Considering that this was my first day of eight, I was a bit discouraged—and concerned about my ability to complete the full 100 miles.

One of the things I had been worried about on this walk was walking too quickly, and I had been hoping to force myself to somehow slow down by becoming aware of my pace. My natural walking speed was pretty fast, especially when I walk alone. Poles enabled me to walk even more speedily.

I wanted to learn how to walk more slowly and take in the scenery, something I often found challenging when out on a day walk. However, my super heavy backpack had done the job of slowing me down on the trail, whether I liked it or not. I don't think I had ever walked this slowly before.

I lamented bringing the iPad, but I knew I'd be thankful for it once I reached my destination in Droxford that evening. I planned to write a little and then read a book. The iPad served both those purposes, but damn, it was heavy. Little did I know that my pack was only to get heavier in the following days when I would need to carry ever-increasing amounts of water on the trail due to the heat and lack of water taps to refill my bottles.

On numerous occasions throughout this first day, I mentally reviewed the contents of my backpack and my packing list. Aside from the third pair of socks that I had decided to bring just in case, and my third pair of underwear, there wasn't much else I could have left behind. I did bring a long-sleeved shirt to use if it got chilly in the mornings, but this now appeared to be a waste: the weather was so hot that I probably wouldn't use it even once on my journey. What I didn't know at that time was that it would come in handy the following day, and every day for the rest of my week—but not for the reason that I had initially brought it.

It was the iPad that had pushed my pack over the weight

limit; I knew it was. I made a mental note to make an actual note to leave the thing behind on my next trip the following year. There was no way I'd carry that iPad and small keyboard again. One day was enough to learn the lesson. I was convinced the iPad was the item that pushed my pack weight over the limit. What I didn't realize was that it wasn't the iPad—it was the heat that was slowing me down.

I reluctantly heaved myself up from the garden bench, brought my glass and bottle back into the pub, and headed back off on the trail. I continued to consume water like never before on my walks. I had drunk almost two liters by the time I happily came across a surprise South Downs Way water fountain, which was not marked on the map in my guidebook. The water was refreshing and delicious, and I happily filled both of my bottles. I made another mental note to get a larger second bottle for the next day, or perhaps even a third bottle.

Once more, I lamented opting for bottles over a water reservoir, which would have made staying hydrated so much easier. Each time that I realized I was thirsty, I had to contort my arm around the side of my pack to pull out a water bottle. If I had a water reservoir, I could just sip from a tube conveniently located on my pack shoulder strap. Lesson noted—for my next adventure.

The walk had begun on a slightly uphill grade heading toward Cheesefoot Head (England is full of ridiculous place names, and this is just one excellent example of them), before descending a bit and then leveling out for the majority of the walk. It gradually ascended once more toward Beacon Hill, the highest point on this stage of my walk.

England is full of places called Beacon Hill. These are usually the site of an ancient flame beacon, where a fire would be lit inside a flame beacon holder, which was usually situated on top of an elevated location such as a hill. The most well-known examples of these are the beacons used in Elizabethan times to warn of the approaching Spanish Armada, signaling across the land that enemy troops were approaching, alerting defenses.

Shortly after passing Exton Beacon, which was the landmark signaling that the end of this day's walking was near, I took off my pack and sat down alongside the trail on a lush green hillside, taking off my left boot and sock. The ball of my left foot had been bothering me for the last couple of hours, and it felt like I had something in my boot, like a tiny pebble. I was so sure of this that I was shocked to see there was nothing there. I shook out my sock and felt inside it, but there was no stone to be found. I was confused, but I decided to take advantage of the stop, and I rested there on the grassy hillside, enjoying the beautiful views of rolling hills all around.

Now I knew for sure there was not a rock in my boot. I resolved to ignore the pain, which had been distracting me quite a bit for the last part of my walk. From there, the trail descended sharply toward Exton, which was the end of the first stage of walking for Day 1. I was grateful for the downhill trail, exhausted from the walk, and the extra weight of the backpack (*and* tired from the heat). The going downhill took some of the pressure off the parts of my feet that hurt the most and gave me a rest from the pain on the ball of my foot.

One thing I was soon to learn about the South Downs Way was that the trail ran along a high ridge, which meant that most days ended with a downhill walk heading off the ridge and into a village below. This, of course, meant that each day's walk began with a steady uphill hike to get back up onto the ridge the following day. I suppose it made for an excellent warm-up exercise for the day's walk, but for now, I was grateful to be heading downhill.

I finally arrived in the little village of Exton, filled with thatched cottages, which for me, are the greatest of English architectural delights. The village was so charming that it looked like it belonged on a postcard. There was a pub with a large garden and a little ice cream shack, which I longed to stop at for a break. But what I wanted, even more, was to reach my final destination for the day, so I could take a shower and relax. Unfortunately, the inn where I was staying was another two miles off the Way.

I had started my walk on a Saturday, and when I booked accommodation for the journey, there had been no availability in Exton or nearby Meonstoke. After a brief panic, I had explored the surrounding areas on Google Maps and found a place to stay in Droxford. This was another South Downs Way Lesson learned: when planning a long-distance walk like this, try to avoid starting or ending on the weekend. There will be naturally more walkers near the start and the end of the trail, especially when the endpoints of the trail are located in major urban areas, and there will generally be more walkers on the weekend than on a weekday.

After arriving exhausted in Exton, my spirits picked up. It was just two miles down the road to Droxford, and having explicit knowledge of the exact distance left to travel helped me to get my mindset in order. I was focused not on the rest of my journey, but my destination. I got a second wind of energy and headed off, excited about the prospect of a refreshing shower and the chance to put my feet up.

The final two miles from Exton to Droxford, where I was staying at the White Horse Inn, were horrific. The first half was a quiet trail that ran alongside a busy road, and the second half involved a stressful trek at the edge of the road, where I had to jump off into the grass and hedgerows whenever a car came past, which unfortunately was every couple of minutes. By the time I reached Droxford, I was thoroughly stressed out and exhausted. This roadside walk was not an ideal end to my quiet afternoon in Nature.

I forged on through the village of Droxford, which despite

its small size, seemed never to end, until I finally spotted the inn on the other side of the road. I was quickly shown to my room, where I immediately collapsed on the bed before heading to the shower. I was sore and smelly, and all I wanted was to take a shower and change my clothes—and to wash the ones I'd been wearing so they'd be ready (and hopefully dry) for the day after tomorrow.

I'd put together a bizarre clothes drying contraption consisting of three binder clips hooked onto a key ring, which I intended to use to clip my damp clothing to the back of my backpack using a carabiner. With the sun we had on Day 1, I was confident that everything was sure to dry, even if I looked a bit odd, walking around with my laundry hanging off the back of my pack. At that point, I was only mildly concerned about hiking down the trail with my laundry flapping in the breeze. I just wanted to cool off in the shower and put some fresh clothes on.

The Evening

This inn was the most economical place I'd booked along the Way. The room was small and basic, but spotless and good enough for my purposes. All I wanted was a simple, clean place to shower and sleep, and that's what I had ended up with. I shared the bathroom with the other two rooms at the inn, which turned out to not be a problem at all in terms of bathroom traffic. After a quick shower, I washed my clothes in the sink, wrung them out to dry, and then hung them up in my room. This was my first experience with what would become a daily ritual: arrive, shower, wash clothes, and hang them to dry.

After my hygiene and laundry had been taken care of, I prepared to head down to the inn's garden for a curry and to start writing about the day's walk. Everything hurt from the waist down, and my muscles were tired and stiff. This routine was to become a daily experience, as I was soon to learn.

I hobbled painfully downstairs to inquire about dinner, breakfast the following morning, and, most importantly, a taxi back to Exton just after breakfast. I had no intention of braving that road again. Walking it would add two extra miles onto my walk the following day, and it would start the day off with much stress. There was no need to be a purist and walk every step of my journey. After all, I was two miles off the South Downs Way. This road was not technically the Way, and I could allow myself a quick cab ride.

After arranging times for breakfast and a taxi in the morning, I settled into a shady table out in the empty pub garden. I enjoyed a massive plate of creamy lamb curry, with rice, potatoes, salad, and naan. I was starving, and I surprised myself by eating almost everything on the plate. I enjoyed a half-pint of Guinness along with my meal, savoring it as I lingered in the quiet, shady garden after dinner, recording my experience of the day's journey on my iPad.

I didn't trust my memory enough to write everything down upon my return, and I was right to do so. I knew the critical details would be lost, and I thought that if I wrote a little bit each day, the book would be mostly finished upon my return. I would just need to add the appendices with resources and other information, and any reflections that arose later in my journey as I read through the early days of my walk.

It appeared to be a good plan, and it was. It also gave me something to do in the late afternoons and evenings after my walk, and it helped me to reflect on each day on the trail. The writing was the perfect evening and morning activity on the Way.

The garden was beginning to fill with families, which wasn't a surprise as the pub manager had warned me there would be a birthday party that evening. It looked like the entire village had turned out for the event, and I escaped upstairs to rest on my bed. After a full day on the trail, I had grown used to the peace of the South Downs Way. Even though the start of the trail had more walkers and cyclists than I had been expecting, it was still a relatively small amount of people compared to the turnout of the party.

I had no desire for people or for noise that evening. Unfortunately, my room's single window looked out on the pub garden, which pulsated with the sound of music and drunken conversation. I read for a little while, then listened to music on my phone before plugging everything in to charge overnight before turning off the lights. I was so tired that the party noise soon faded into the background. I didn't even bother to use the earplugs I had brought with me.

I reflected on Pure Joy, my theme for the day. Despite all the little annoyances and aches and pains, it was such a pleasure to be back out in Nature on a long walk. My almost constant irritation was secondary to the joy of being out in the countryside, walking the Way. Walking in Nature is one of those things that makes my heart sing. It lights up my soul. So yes, I experienced pure joy on Day 1—despite myself.

DAY 2

L ichen–Groundedness was the theme for my second day of walking. Groundedness is, of course, the state of being grounded—but there are different meanings for this word. The more "alternative" definition involves getting in direct contact with the earth, like when we walk barefoot on the ground. It's also called "earthing." It's believed to help increase energy levels and improve our overall wellbeing. The more traditional meaning of the word "grounded" is that of a person who makes good decisions and says sensible things: someone who is wise, responsible, and clear-headed. Which definition would prove to be the appropriate one for this day's walk?

The Morning

I had been so exhausted the evening before that even the loud party downstairs in the courtyard couldn't keep me from falling asleep quickly. I slept deeply throughout the night, waking up briefly to a bird singing outside my window at 6 am, and then drifting back to sleep until one minute before my alarm went off at eight. This was a novelty for me; I never wake up before my alarm.

As I dragged myself out of bed, I realized—without surprise —that everything hurt. It was usual for my legs and feet to ache the day after a long walk. But now my shoulders hurt as well, and I had this horrible chafing on my lower back from the pack. Desperate for a quick solution, I resolved to use the long-sleeved base layer that was too hot for this weather to tie around my waist in the hopes that it would provide a bit of cushioning. This ended up being the perfect solution, and I continued to use the shirt in this manner every day for the remainder of my journey.

I slathered arnica cream all over the aching bits and headed downstairs for breakfast, which I had been unable to order before 9 am. I had been hoping for an earlier start, but it was a Sunday morning, and this was as good as I could get. My taxi was supposed to pick me up at 10 to take me back to Exton, and I was thrilled at the prospect of avoiding the long walk down that busy road.

Never before had I eaten a full English breakfast with such relish. I was starving, despite the massive curry I had devoured the evening before, and I was grateful for the cooked breakfast. I was also alone in the pub, which I much appreciated. Everything was quiet after the busy party the night before. After finishing my meal, I attempted to get an earlier taxi. The official taxi services were closed, but local drivers were available. However, none could pick me up before ten. This was another lesson in flexibility: clearly, there was some reason why I needed to get a later start this morning. Or perhaps I just needed to learn to relax and learn to be patient.

I ever so briefly entertained the idea of walking back to Exton so I could get an earlier start, but that was just a fleeting thought before I quickly recalled the stress of walking along-side the road the day before. I was here for a relaxing, meditative walk in Nature, not a stressful walk down a busy road. I resolved to be patient—a virtue that I lacked—and wait for the taxi.

My mind drifted to my weekly Akashic Records reading, which had popped into my email inbox just before midnight. The Akashic Records are, according to Wikipedia, a "compendium of thoughts, events, and emotions believed by theosophists to be encoded in a non-physical plane of existence known as the astral plane." It's a virtual encyclopedia for each person in the world—including information on our past, present, and future lives.

I regularly subscribed to a service provided by Vickie Young of Medicine Dream Healing, who connects to your Akashic records every week on Sunday and sends you a short personal reading, along with an oracle card that she draws to provide more information on the topic. Not surprisingly (though I must admit I'm *always* surprised when my Record Keepers know precisely what I'm up to), the message was about walking.

An excerpt:

"Holly, you are discovering your roots! When you travel countryside to countryside you are walking the paths of your ancestors. They each sing a song for you. Do you ever hear it? You might hear music or not...

They are urging you to develop a love for them...to discover where they came from and the missions they served. They are asking you to help them complete their missions because of various reasons they could not. Listen in the wind. The answers lie there.

They speak in the wind and send messages to you about this...just listen."

I set the intention to remind myself of this message throughout the day's walk, as I also contemplated the day's theme: Groundedness. Ever since I moved to England, I had felt a deep connection to this land. Someone once mentioned that perhaps it was due to my ancestors being from here as if this were kind of a homecoming for me. My father's side of the family was English and Welsh, so at some level, this makes sense. But I'd never really given it much thought until this Akashic reading. I was curious as to what messages would come through to me on my walks throughout the week.

As for Groundedness, that had come up in the previous week's Akashic reading. I was in a time of transition, and I would receive messages about what would come next. They urged me to get out in Nature and go walking whenever I felt like I needed to get grounded. And here I was, out walking 100 miles on the South Downs Way. There would surely be plenty of opportunities for me to get grounded not just this day, but also throughout the entire week.

I was curious as to how things would go for me. This second stage of the walk looked very different from the previous day, with more points of interest along the way, including the Queen Elizabeth Country Park. This meant there would be more opportunities to fill up my water and get snacks if needed, though I was also hoping to eat my way through the heavy snacks of nuts and dried fruit that I had packed. The concept of weight had taken on a whole new meaning with this backpack, and I had begun to consider the nuts and dried fruit to be an unnecessary addition to my pack.

Water was one thing I was concerned about. From the start of the walk the previous day, I had been very much aware of how inconvenient it was to get a drink of water. I was carrying my two bottles on the sides of my pack. This meant that I had to contort my arm around to grab a bottle, or I had to take off my pack entirely—something I tried to avoid at all costs, as it was often a grave reminder of just how much weight I was carrying. My first day on the South Downs had made me question every little thing that I was carrying on my back.

Before I had departed, I was in a big debate: water bladder or bottles? When I went on shorter walks with a lighter pack, it was no problem to carry bottles on the sides and just pop off my little daypack to reach them. But it was a whole other story with this big, heavy pack, and from the very start of my walk the previous day, I had wished I had brought a water bladder instead. I resolved that would be the first thing I would buy when I returned home from my walk. My pack had a special compartment to hold a water reservoir, so that would make things easier.

Despite having drunk more than two liters of water yesterday, I realized that it just wasn't enough. At home, I would regularly drink at least two liters, when in the comfort of my office, and I would end up using the toilet several times a day. The day before, out on the Way, I had gone once, then once again at the inn. I was not drinking enough water.

I resolved to drink more water on this day, as the unexpected heat was demanding a much higher water consumption than I was used to. I was mainly concerned to keep hydrated because I was out alone on the trail, with no one to take care of me if I got into trouble, and no way to call for help. I was very much aware of the need to take care of myself on this journey.

The Walk

The thirteen miles from Exton to Buriton (plus a two-mile detour I made when I got lost), wind around Old Winchester Hill, one of the best examples of an Iron Age hill-fort site in the south of England. From there, the trail heads down to Meon Springs, a fishing base where you can get refreshments. Then it passes the Sustainability Centre across from the former HMS Mercury (a former Naval Signal School that was demolished to build luxury homes), and finally, the Queen Elizabeth Country Park. This second stage, which culminates in the village of

Buriton, alternates between glorious, remote Nature and small centers of civilization, where walkers can get drinks and snacks.

It was an absolute pleasure to get a taxi back to the little village of Exton, where I took up the South Downs Way once again. I must have thanked the cab driver at least three times; I was so grateful to be driven back down that dangerous road. I hopped out of the taxi with my pack, my bag of poles, and a small paper bag containing the sandwich the inn had packed for me. This was one good thing about the B&Bs and inns located along the Way: most of them are used to catering for walkers and can pack a simple lunch if requested in advance.

After the taxi had driven off, I set down my pack to reorganize things: first, I pulled out my bizarre contraption with all of my damp clothes hanging off binder clips and attached it to the outside of my pack. I then placed my sandwich inside, carefully arranged on top of everything else, and after closing up my backpack, I was ready to go. I hoisted it up onto my back and fastened first the hip belt, then the sternum strap.

The weather was much cooler than the day before: the sky was overcast, and there was just a hint of a breeze. I was grateful for the lower temperature, and I recognized this to be perfect British walking weather, which was a surprising realization to come to since I had always yearned for sunny days to walk. So far, the South Downs Way was proving to be full of lessons and new insights.

The trail started clear enough, with obvious signposts along the Way. Soon I was walking along what appeared to be an old railway path: it was wide, perfectly flat and smooth, and overgrown with trees, forming a perfectly straight, leafy green tunnel. These old rail lines make for gorgeous walking trails, though it's hard not to mourn the loss of so many miles of rural railways in the 1960s.

British Rail was losing £140 million a year when Dr.

Richard Beeching took over as chairman of the British Transport Commission. His solution was to drastically reduce the number of rail lines in Britain, which led to the closing of more than 4,500 miles of track, 2,128 stations, and the loss of more than 67,000 jobs. The rail cuts began in 1962 and ended in the early 1970s, and many small villages were left without a convenient mode of public transportation. Buses are often few and far between.

Droxford, the village where I had stayed the previous night, was one such example of these closures: the station had opened in 1903 and then closed in 1962. The station was, however, not without its historical moments: in 1944, Allied leaders, including Churchill, Eisenhower, and de Gaulle met in a train carriage at Droxford station to discuss the imminent D-Day invasion. Less than 20 years later, that station was no longer in operation.

The shade of the overgrown rail line added to the refreshing aspect of the morning's walk, which was very welcome after the previous day's heat. I was all alone, with no one in front of me or behind me, and it felt great to be walking through this wide green tunnel by myself. There was no hint of the previous day's irritations. They had bubbled up and out, and had been replaced by a sense of peace—or perhaps it was Groundedness?

There was some work being done on the Way because ever since the end of the first day, there were signs marked "Temporary South Downs Way." The temporary signs continued, and I reached a point where this temporary trail split into two parts once again: a footpath for walkers and a bridleway for cyclists and horse riders. I opted for the walkers' path, hoping once again to avoid cyclists, and I headed down some stairs to a point where the trail seemed to disappear: the track was overgrown.

I retraced my steps back up the stairs and decided to choose the bridleway, but even that wasn't clear. It followed an overgrown dry creek bed, but it was so tricky to navigate that it was clearly not a bridleway. I went back once more, and decided to take my chances on a trail marked simply "Bridleway." I was nervous that it didn't specifically mention the South Downs Way. I walked on in doubt for about a half-hour before I saw another sign for the Way, after which point I allowed myself to fully relax and enjoy the journey, knowing with confidence that I was on the right path. I had been afraid of getting lost again and adding more distance to my journey, as I had at the start of the previous day.

The Way wound up and around fields of grain and flax, which glowed a soft purple-blue from a distance. From there, it was up, up, up to Old Winchester Hill, which is home to what is considered to be one of the finest Iron Age hill-fort sites in the south of England, even though it has never been fully excavated. It is both a Site of Special Scientific Interest and a National Nature Reserve.

Several Bronze Age barrows (mounds of earth and stones raised over gravesites) dating from between 4,500 and 3,500 BCE can be found within the hill-fort. The fort itself is believed to be of Iron Age in origin, dating back to sometime between 600-300 BCE. I took a brief detour to read the information signs, which pointed out the different tumuli and other remains of the old hill fort. I was concerned about not making the day's walk longer than I needed to, so I didn't explore further.

Because this was a well-known and easily accessible area, I crossed paths with a few random people: two women walking in the opposite direction who seemed to be out on a quick morning walk, and later a couple who were exploring the archaeological site on Old Winchester Hill. I wasn't in the least bit annoyed to see other people out walking, which was a massive improvement in my mood from the previous day. I was happy that I had finally relaxed. I had become more flexible in dealing with my surroundings. I felt like I was settling into the rhythm of the trail.

The path continued through the National Nature Reserve, and it was at this point that it started sprinkling. I can't even call it rain, it was so light, but it did mean that I had to unhook my drying clothes and hide them inside my pack. It sprinkled on and off for the next half hour, leading me to stop at least three times to remove my clothes once again and then store them back in my pack. I was unsure as to whether my clothes would ever be dry for the following day's walk, which was mildly worrying.

By this time, I was approaching Meon Springs Fishing Lodge & Cafe, a fly-fishing school and base located on the headwaters of the River Meon. The center offers fly-fishing on four lakes and also accommodation in yurts and huts. The cafe provides simple breakfasts, snacks during the day, and hot and cold drinks. My guidebook had mentioned it was an excellent place to stop for refreshments, and the signs outside confirmed this, so I headed inside to take a look. Seated at a table just inside the door was the couple I had passed several times the previous day. I was shocked to see them, as I hadn't come across them at all that morning. They must have left much earlier than I had. We spoke for a few minutes, discussing where we had each stayed the previous night, and then they got up and headed back to the trail.

I bought a new bottle of water and sat down for a quick cup of hot tea. After taking advantage of the bathroom, I was off again. I wasn't back on the trail for more than three minutes before I came across the other small group of people I had seen the previous day: the two women and a man. They struck up a conversation with me about Pacerpoles. They had the same ones and were surprised to see me with them, as well, as they're a unique type of walking pole. We chatted for a few minutes (it seemed that the obligatory conversation on the Way centered around three main topics: where one had stayed the night before, where one was walking to that day, and of course the quality of the weather), and then I was off up the hill.

My body had warmed up to the walking, and the morning's aches and pains were gone. My energy levels were high on this second day of walking, and my pack felt much lighter than the previous day, which seemed miraculous. I was starting to feel a bit self-conscious about walking with my underwear hanging off the back of my pack, and eventually, I ended up removing it and putting it in the mesh pocket of my backpack. It was almost dry, anyway. The sports bra flapping off the back of my pack didn't bother me, and neither did my socks. It was the underwear because it was lacy, and it was apparent what it was. Of course, most people don't walk around with their panties flapping in the breeze on their backpack. This was the South Downs Way, not London, but I still felt the need to behave somewhat decently.

I forged on up the hill until I came to a four-way signpost. Straight ahead was a footpath to East Meon, and to the left was a bridleway that also led there. I chose the footpath and headed downhill, winding around past Garston Dairy until I came out on the road. There was no South Downs Way sign, which was my first indication that I was lost. I knew I had walked a mile, as the signpost had indicated one mile to East Meon.

I was so confused. I had no idea where I had gone wrong. I consulted my guidebook, and quickly determined that East Meon was most definitely not on the South Downs Way; it was a short walk off the Way. My guidebook indicated that it was a half-hour detour from the path and was well worth a stop for a lunch break. The small village is thought to date back to 400-600 AD, as part of a Royal Manor belonging to King Alfred the Great. Today, the village is home to the 900-year-old All Saints Church, built after the Norman Conquest.

Despite my proximity to the village, I was not keen to make

a cultural detour that afternoon, and I turned around and headed back up the hill to my last known point on the Way: the four-armed signpost. As I walked, I tried to evaluate where I had gone wrong, and I honestly had no idea. I was annoyed to be adding an extra two miles to my walk. The day's journey was already an estimated twelve miles, plus an additional mile and a half to my accommodation, which was once more off the Way.

When I returned to the signpost, it was instantly very, very clear where I should have turned: as I said, it was a four-fingered post. The path I hadn't even considered, or even seen as far as I could remember, was the one that clearly said South Downs Way. Coming from my original direction, it was off to the right. I couldn't understand how I had missed such a clear sign. This was another lesson of the Way: pay attention to signposts, and read *every single finger* on the sign before proceeding.

Because I hadn't read the sign clearly, I had just added two more miles to my already long day. This was not encouraging. The only good news was that it had stopped sprinkling and the path had become another cool green tunnel, bordered by shrubs and trees. The walk from there followed a very long uphill slope for what seemed like ages. I was starting to get tired, and I was annoyed with myself for making such an obvious mistake. I just couldn't let it go. Eventually, I reached the top of the hill, with views all over the South Downs and bright pink foxgloves in bloom alongside the trail. It was gorgeous enough to help me let go of my annoyance.

From there, it was all downhill, but in a good way, until I passed the Sustainability Centre, an independent learning and study center for sustainability and a social enterprise charity located near East Meon. The Sustainability Centre also offers accommodation in the form of lodge rooms, camping, yurts, and tipis and refreshment in the way of the Beech Cafe. It was already 2 pm, and I still wasn't the least bit hungry after that full English breakfast in the morning. I always underestimate the amount of time that it takes to digest a full English breakfast, and I had been concerned that I wouldn't have enough to eat along the Way with the small sandwich the pub had made for me.

However, it had been five hours since I'd had breakfast that morning, so I decided it was time to eat something. I sat on a bench at the side of the quiet road and quickly ate my chicken tikka sandwich. I entertained the idea of heading into the Sustainability Centre to visit their cafe, but I just couldn't justify yet another diversion. Not after my two-mile mistake earlier. I ate quickly and took advantage of the recycling bins in the parking lot of the Sustainability Centre to throw away my sandwich's packaging before heading back down the Way.

There were fewer cyclists on this part of the path—though there was one who had passed me twice and courteously rung his bell from a reasonable distance both times. I thanked him the first time, I was so grateful for the warning. Shortly after he passed me for the second time, another cyclist went past, and as usual, I didn't hear him until he was just behind me. I jumped, startled, and then quickly leaped out of his way. He thanked me and then laughed at my reaction, which I can imagine must have appeared exaggerated. Surely I can't be the only walker who gets startled by cyclists? But at least today I could laugh at my reaction, rather than get annoyed by the cyclists.

From there, it was down a quiet country lane and into the Queen Elizabeth Country Park, which is a 2,000-acre country park full of open access woodlands and downs. The forest within the park was mostly planted in the 1930s and consists mainly of beech trees. Several long-distance footpaths run through the park, of which the South Downs Way is just one. On a clear day, the Isle of Wight can be seen from the top of Butser Hill. This part of the trail involved a smooth downhill slope with extensive views all around. It was a Sunday, and there were more people out, making it apparent that I was approaching civilization once again.

Near the bottom of the hill, I crossed paths with a man and his son, who were heading westward. They planned to arrive at Exton that evening. It was already 3 pm, and they were discouraged at having ten miles yet to go. I did a rough calculation in my head, and I realized they wouldn't make it there until seven or eight in the evening, which I thought was a little risky. I told them I was walking to Buriton, and they were encouraging, saying it was only about two miles and just "over that hill," indicating a large hill on the other side of the A3. This was both a good sign and a bad sign, as it meant I had another large hill to walk up, and I was already feeling tired, thanks to my unplanned detour.

I headed under the A3 via a tunnel and up into the other side of the Queen Elizabeth Country Park, which the A3 splits in two. There was a sign for the Visitor Centre and cafe, and part of me desperately wanted to rest for a bit, yet at the same time, I was so close to my day's destination that another part of me just wanted to arrive. In the end, I opted to take a rest.

After a quick trip to the bathroom (no outdoors pit stops for me on this second day of walking), I went to the café, and after a long debate, bought a ginger beer. I don't usually drink sugary sodas, but a ginger beer sounded refreshing. When I sat down in the courtyard, I saw the couple I had been crossing paths with since the day before. We struck up a conversation, and it turned out that they were walking the Way in two-day stages, on the weekends. This was their first weekend on the South Downs.

I was grateful to have the time to do the full length of the walk all at once, mostly because it seemed immensely satisfying to me to walk an entire trail from point to point in one go, something I had never done before. They mentioned that they wished they had the time to do it all at once. After a few minutes' rest, I said goodbye and was back up and off to the trail. The Queen Elizabeth Country Park also contains several graded mountain biking trails that wind through the thick woodland, and the Way now headed along these shady trails. It was very different from the open grassy fields on the other side of the country park.

As I had imagined when viewing the hill from afar, the trail headed steadily upwards until I felt sure I must have gone too far. I asked a cyclist heading in the opposite direction whether I was on the way to Buriton, and he confirmed that I was and that it wasn't too far away, perhaps just a mile. By this point, I was exhausted, and it soon turned out that he had overestimated the distance as the path shortly began to slope downhill, and I quickly arrived at the Halls Hill car park, where I exited the Queen Elizabeth Country Park. This park was a clear landmark on my map, and it made it easier for me to find where I was located in relation to that night's accommodation.

From this point, I followed a combination of my guidebook's map and the B&B's directions to reach the center of Buriton, which was a pretty little village with a church dating back to the 12th century. Unfortunately, I was too tired to head up for a visit. Buriton is also home to two pubs, but no village shop, which is an important detail if you're passing through on the Way.

From Buriton, I then veered off toward the B&B, which was on the road to Nursted. I was headed to Nursted Farm, a family-run working farm offering bed and breakfast accommodations in its 18th-century farmhouse. The farm's rural location boasted viewings of deer, pheasants, hares, and foxes during the daytime hours and owls and bats at night. Just the kind of place I love: surrounded by wildlife.

The Bray family has been living at the farm for over a hundred years, and Andrew, the current farmer, is the fourth generation of the family to farm the land. His parents, Gordon and Mary, run the B&B and are also involved in the farm work. The farm grows cereal crops, including wheat, barley, oats, and rapeseed as well as sheep, including 440 ewes and 16 rams.

I checked my guidebook, which indicated that the farm was a 30-minute walk from Buriton, and I compared it to the B&B's directions, which said one mile. I lamented my decision to once again stay so far off the South Downs Way. My only consolation was that my guidebook had spoken so highly of the B&B, which sounded magical. Nevertheless, I was looking forward to arriving and settling in.

Still exhausted, aching, and tired, I plodded down the road toward the farm, checking my watch every few minutes to see how much time was left. It occurred to me that walking was so much like life and business: in the same way that we create an itinerary for our walking journey, we set ourselves goals in other parts of our lives. The main difference, as far as I could see, was that it's much easier to fall short on our goals, whereas I had no choice but to walk until I reached my destination for that day. I couldn't just crash on the side of the road and sleep in the bushes for the night.

Suddenly, an older man in a small Ford Ka pulled over and asked me if I was headed to the farm. I said I was, and he told me to hop in the car and he would drive me the rest of the way. I was so tired that I didn't bat an eye. It turned out he was Gordon, the owner of the farm. The drive was much, much longer than I had expected it to be, and I was so grateful that he had stopped to pick me up. I realized that I would have been exhausted if I had had to walk that extra bit.

It was a reminder that sometimes when we least expect it, people show up to help us reach our destination or achieve our goal. The funny thing is that when he offered me a ride, I considered telling him, "no, thanks," feeling like it was somehow cheating to get a lift to my B&B, even though this wasn't officially part of the South Downs Way. I've always been terrible about asking for help or accepting it when it's offered to me, and yet I'm honestly not sure how I would have made it that last mile or so. I was so tired and achy.

The Evening

Upon arrival, Gordon indicated that I should knock on the door, and his wife Mary would be there to let me in. She responded quickly to my knock, and after taking off my boots and leaving them in the front hallway, I was shown to my room. Mary asked me if I wanted a cup of tea, and I gratefully replied in the affirmative. After dropping everything off in my room, I headed downstairs for tea.

The other three guests were there as well: a single woman in her sixties who was walking the Way from east to west, and a couple—Martin and Maggie—who were walking the same direction as I was. They, too, were on their second day of walking and had stayed at the Sustainability Centre the previous night. All three had arrived not long before I had, though they hadn't had the good fortune to get a ride part of the way there. I realized how lucky my timing was, as Gordon had been heading back from a concert at the church.

We shared stories about our journeys thus far and compared our list of places we each wanted to walk in the future. We talked about the book and the film *Wild*. We discussed what it was like to walk in the US compared to England (that bit of the conversation mostly centered around bears and how lucky we were not to have them in Britain). I'm such a solo walker, and I can be quite a hermit in my daily life, so I was stunned how much I enjoyed our conversation as we all drank our tea and nibbled our homemade biscuits. It was so satisfying to sit with three other walkers and talk about our experience of the South Downs Way and our other walking plans. My fellow walkers were delightful.

The B&B, unfortunately, didn't serve dinner, though the owners offered to drive us to nearby Petersfield if we wanted. We would, however, have to find our own way back, and I was not thrilled with the idea of another walk, this time in the twilight. Plus, I was exhausted and couldn't imagine leaving the farm, even if I did manage to get a taxi back. We all four opted to stay in and just eat whatever snacks we each had, which was fine with me. I was a bit concerned about not having a proper dinner, especially after the giant curry I had eaten the evening before, but I figured I would survive.

I showered, changed, washed my walking clothes, and hung them up in my room for the first part of the drying process. I was delighted that my tactic of tying my long-sleeved shirt to my waist had helped with the chafing, and I planned to do the same the following day. Then I slathered myself with arnica cream on all the aching bits and settled in to write, nibbling on the dried bananas and cashews I had in my pack. I was surprised that I wasn't hungry, considering how much I had eaten the evening before.

What about Groundedness, my theme for the day? I supposed I was feeling more grounded, at least at times. Even at my lowest, most difficult points of the day, my pack felt considerably lighter than the previous day, which was such a relief. I had already eaten some of my dried bananas, but that wasn't enough to make a difference in the weight. It seemed I was simply getting used to walking with a heavy pack.

I was also beginning to realize that my pack fit my body very well: I was aware of the pack's weight when pulling it on or taking it off, but when it was on my body, it felt perfectly comfortable. Except for my aching feet and the chafing from the first day, my pack was causing no other pain, not even in my shoulders. That it fit so well was no small miracle, considering that I had purchased my pack online, without trying it on in a store. And I hadn't even used it to do a practice walk before embarking on the South Downs. I was very much aware of how lucky I was that it had worked out perfectly.

And more importantly, I was settling into the rhythm of walking the Way: I was no longer bothered by crossing paths with other walkers, even when they were going the same direction as I was. I was also no longer irritated by cyclists, even though they startled me whenever they came up behind me without warning. It was as though all my initial irritation from the first morning had bubbled up and out, and I felt a sense of peace on the following days.

When I reflected on my disappointment at having embarked on a two-mile, unintentional detour, I realized that even then, I had only been mildly irritated with myself. It seemed that I was relaxing into the Way and becoming kinder to myself with my mistakes. I also understood that getting lost that day had been my second lesson on paying attention to maps and signs. The signpost was very clearly marked where I had gotten lost, and I just hadn't paid enough attention to it. This day had also been a lesson in the traditional sense of the word "groundedness"—I had learned to pay attention on the trail so I could make wise, responsible, more clear-headed decisions.

DAY 3

BURITON TO COCKING: 11+3/4 MILES (18+1.2 KM)

ilk Thistle–Courage was the theme for this day's walk, which sounded exciting and adventurous, but also a bit ominous. What would I need courage for? Would I receive a lesson in courage while out on the trail? I was a bit concerned.

What was going to happen on this day, my third on the South Downs? What awaited me on the Way? Tiredness? Hunger? Thirst? I mentally prepared myself for the worst (probably not a good idea when embarking on an adventure). The good news was that the day's walk was only eleven miles (18 km.), which would be my shortest day yet, assuming my B&B wasn't too far off the main trail and provided that I didn't get lost like I had the day before. I looked forward to having a slightly more leisurely walk—or so I thought.

The Morning

Despite being physically tired, it had taken what seemed like ages to fall asleep, which was unusual for me. For the past couple of months, I'd been able to fall asleep quickly and easily. The bed was comfortable, and the farm and farmhouse were quiet. There was no reason for me to have trouble falling asleep. I had reflected on the day's walk when writing it all up on my iPad, so the problem wasn't that I had too many things going on in my head. I couldn't understand it.

After what felt like minutes, I woke up and peeked at the alarm: it was just before five, so I went back to sleep. I had set my alarm for seven intending to have breakfast at eight. I slept for what felt like hours, then woke just before six and couldn't get back to sleep, so I gave up.

In between the two times I woke up, I had a dream that my alarm hadn't gone off, and I had ended up waking at 8:40. The other guests had already had breakfast and had headed out to the trail, which left me feeling disappointed, as I didn't want to be late getting back on the road again. In my dream, the B&B owner had left me a tiny bowl of what appeared to be cream of wheat or some other gritty, grainy cereal. There was also what looked like half a hamburger inside a pita pocket, accompanied by a few sad fries. There was more to the dream, but it's not worth exploring in detail (in it, I discovered that my parents had also moved to this area...from the US, though they hadn't yet mentioned it to me, and strangely they, too, had little food at home). Perhaps I was dreaming of food because I hadn't had a proper meal the previous night, but I didn't feel hungry. In any case, I gave up trying to go back to sleep after that dream and got out of bed.

I was concerned about having to walk another full day on what seemed to be such little sleep. I had gone to bed just after ten and tried to calculate how much tossing and turning I had done before actually following asleep, so I could estimate how many hours of sleep I had had. Yet somehow, I felt rested and refreshed, ready to be awake and to get going with the day. It was confusing because I'm one of those people who needs eight full hours of sleep.

I was looking forward to a good breakfast after having nibbled on nuts and dried fruit the night before, and I was also worried about lunch that day. I had forgotten to ask Mary if she could put together a sandwich to take with me, and I was afraid that lunch would also be out of the question. From the map I had of Buriton, I knew that there was no village store, nowhere to buy anything for lunch, and from the maps I had of today's stretch across the South Downs, there were no snack shops or refreshment places like there had been the day before. Some stages of the Way had water taps, pubs, and stores, and others had nothing but remote woodland and farmland. Each day was very different on the trail.

Fortunately, the day started with the most delightful breakfast ever, served family-style around a huge dining table downstairs in the farmhouse. We were served brown bread, a selection of cereals, fruit, and yogurt, and a full cooked breakfast. Gordon went back and forth between the dining room and the kitchen, bringing us each stage of our breakfast as Mary prepared it. Once again, I enjoyed the conversation with my companions around the table and felt sad to be saying goodbye to them once we all started back on the Way. I knew that I would never again see the woman who was walking from east to west, and I wasn't sure about the couple who was walking in the same direction as I was. As it turned out, we'd end up crossing paths every single day until the end of our journey. It ended up being one of those pleasant daily South Downs reunions: running into them on the trail or at a B&B. There's something satisfying about having a shared purpose with other people, and then comparing notes on our experiences along the way.

Thankfully, I was able to get a small cheese and pickle

sandwich to take on my walk. I was very aware of the fact that there were no pubs or cafes on this stretch of the Way, not even a water tap to fill up bottles. I had to be completely self-sufficient in the food and water department, and I wanted to make sure I had enough to make it to Cocking, my next destination along the South Downs.

The Walk

This stage of the Way, eleven miles between Buriton and Cocking, follows tracks along the top of the South Downs, and is relatively wooded and shady for the first part of the trail, before opening up after South Harting, which is just off the Way. From there, the path opens up into rolling hills of the Harting Down National Trust property, over Beacon Hill (yes, another one), then alongside the Monkton Estate and over Cocking Down, before finally descending into the village of Cocking, which is less than a mile off the Way.

The four of us dreaded the thought of a two-mile walk back to the South Downs Way, and fortunately, our hostess was kind enough to drive us most of the way. As I mentioned, three of us were headed east; one was headed west. Mary indicated that those of us heading east should head down a small path near the road and eventually turn right.

We were a bit unclear as to where exactly we were supposed to turn right, but when we came across a byway, we decided to turn down it. It was a damp, leafy green tunnel of trees, with what looked like a small stream running down parts of the path. It was crisp and refreshing, even though much of it was uphill. I was grateful for my Pacerpoles, which helped me to prevent slipping in the mud.

None of us was entirely sure that we were on the right path to get back on the South Downs Way, and I reflected on how my walking pace had become a bit hesitant. I noticed that during the times when I was clear that I was walking on the right path, I would stride forward with confidence and a steady rhythm. It was so much easier to move forward with determination and confidence when I knew for sure I was on the right path.

We soon came back out on the Way, turning left down a quiet country road. The detour had saved us about a mile of walking down this same lane. We now headed confidently down this paved road, which was lined with copper beech trees, clearly signposted as the South Downs Way. The sun was shining, and the copper beech trees were glorious, rising alongside the road with their vast crowns of deep purple leaves. It was another one of those beautiful days to be out walking in England. When the sun shines, it often feels like paradise to be outdoors.

I was concerned about walking with the couple I had met the afternoon before at the farm. I liked walking with them, but I wasn't sure whether they wanted to walk alone or not, and I did want to do most of the day's walking by myself. We soon fell into a rhythm of ebb and flow: I sometimes stopped to take a photo with my phone, and they would carry on. Sometimes Martin would stop to take a picture with his camera, and Maggie and I would go on. One of us would rest, and the other two would go ahead. It all flowed naturally.

Eventually, I passed them both and continued on just a little ahead of them. I wanted to start recording some of my thoughts (I had brought a small audio recorder with me to keep track of my observations throughout the day, so I could then transcribe them in the evenings). Still, I felt a bit silly, pulling out the recorder in front of them. At one point, I noticed I had gained a bit of distance ahead of them, and I brought out the recorder from my pack to make two brief recordings.

It occurred to me that this was perhaps a small act of courage. While I've gotten much, much better over the years, I do sometimes worry about what others might think of me, even with silly unimportant things like recording my observations along the walk. It was easy enough to explain what I was doing if either of them asked me, and yet I had been so worried about doing it. I continued along, taking out the recorder every once in a while to make verbal notes on the journey. I was farther ahead of the couple, but close enough to still see them if I turned around.

Physically and emotionally, I felt great. I found it surprising how my body recovered each evening and night. Every morning I had started full of energy and ready to get back on the trail. Either the arnica cream was performing miracles in helping my aching muscles to recover each night, or my body was simply healing itself on its own. I wasn't sure how long I could keep this up, but for now, it was working perfectly.

I forged ahead, and at one point, realized that I could no longer see them behind me. I assumed that I had just gained a bit of distance between us, but that ended up being the last time I saw them that day until the afternoon, a couple of hours after I arrived in Cocking. At this point, I assumed they must have taken a detour off the Way to Uppark House or South Harting, but later that day, I learned they just had a leisurely walk with many photo stops.

The Way was full of ups and downs on this third day, as it had been since the start of the trail in Winchester. I entered the National Trust property of Harting Down and continued on a wide, open path along a grassy hill. Harting Down is a 550-acre common, which forms part of the Sussex Downs Area of Outstanding Natural Beauty. Its highest point rises to 751 feet (229 meters) and boasts spectacular panoramic views. Archaeological studies suggest that the area was first occupied around 5,000 years ago.

As the path sloped down into a small valley, I saw a large hill loom up in front of me: Beacon Hill, another Iron Age hillfort built around 500 BCE. I hoped that the South Downs Way didn't go straight up the hill, as I could see a trail going straight up it. When I approached the five armed signpost, I was relieved to see that the Way went to the right, around the hill.

I was already starting to feel tired, and it wasn't even noon. So much for my regained sense of energy! I saw a huge leafy tree to the side of the trail, and plopped myself down under it, taking off my pack and laying down my poles. I pulled out my water bottle and my guidebook as I rested, leafing through the maps of this day's walk to see just how far I had come. It felt like I hadn't been walking for very long, yet I had just seen a sign that indicated only seven miles to Cocking, my destination for that day.

I went through my notes and remembered once more that today's was a shorter walk: just eleven miles. My guidebook stated that the path I was currently on was the official trail of the South Downs Way, and that climbing Beacon Hill made for a shorter route, but that it was "more fun." I looked both ways. The official path made a wide loop around Beacon Hill, and it appeared that the trail up and over the hill was indeed much shorter. I was hesitant to stray from the official South Downs Way as I wanted to walk every inch of its 100 miles, but according to the guidebook, the hill was more fun. How could I turn down that opportunity? I stood up and retraced my steps back toward the base of Beacon Hill.

I'm not sure that "fun" is the right word for it. I huffed and puffed up the side of Beacon Hill, stopping to rest halfway up, at which point I was passed by a group of about eight runners, who charged up the hill in the sun and heat. They quickly passed me and continued onward, disappearing down the other side of the hill. Reaching the top, I turned around, admiring the view and taking a 360-degree video before heading down the other side.

Because of its elevation, Beacon Hill had been home to a station in the shutter telegraph chain from 1796 to 1816. The semaphore telegraph system consisted of a chain of buildings, each located on a prominent hill and each bearing a series of eight shutters on their roofs. The shutters were opened and closed using levers, with each of the 63 different shutter combinations signifying a different letter or word. Each building in the chain could be seen from the next in line. In this way, a message was passed along the chain. This system was invented in 1792 in France by Claude Chappe and was popular in the late eighteenth to the early nineteenth century.

It was Monday, and the walk had been pretty solitary thus far until I reached the Harting Down National Trust property, but because there was a car park at the edge of the property, the easy access meant more people. I passed a few walkers and saw three more off in the distance. But it wasn't until I crossed to the other side of Beacon Hill that I was passed by two cyclists, the only two I would see that day. This day's walk was a solitary one, and that didn't bother me one bit.

There was another small hill to climb shortly after Beacon Hill, and then the path began to wind uphill yet again as it headed into a forest. It was a gradual slope, and I was surprised at how easily I was able to steadily climb it, despite being tired from the morning's previous hills. Still, I felt like it was time for a rest, and I resolved to take a break for lunch as soon as I reached the top.

I was able to find a flat, shady spot to enjoy my small cheese and pickle sandwich. I was tired, and I had already drunk half my water. It was a hot, sunny day, very much like the first day had been. It seemed that I had chosen the hottest week of the year to walk the South Downs. The weather was very, very un-English.

As it had been since the start of my South Downs journey, getting up from a break was the hardest part. I was always stiff and sore after a rest, and it usually took several minutes to warm up again and get back into the rhythm of walking. This stiffness after a rest usually made me hesitate before stopping for a break, as it was often so painfully hard to start up again. This day, however, would prove to be the day with the most rest breaks thus far, despite it being such a short walk. I wasn't sure whether it was because I was feeling more tired than on previous days, or whether I was simply allowing myself more breaks because I knew I had fewer miles to cover.

There were several minor attractions in a small area: first, a memorial to Joseph Ostermann, a German pilot who was shot down in 1940. Next, Monkton Estate off to the right, which I couldn't see much of, but whose peacocks I could hear screeching through the brush. Finally, the Devil's Jumps off to the left: a series of Bronze Age burial mounds dating back between three and four thousand years. The Devil's Jumps is the finest barrow cemetery located along the South Downs, and the mounds were still very well-formed, though most of them had already been excavated.

The tumuli, or barrows, are laid out in a straight line running approximately southeast to northwest, which is aligned with sunset on Midsummer Day. The five main barrows vary in diameter from 26 to 34 meters, with a height of almost five meters. Two smaller barrows are located nearby. Trees had been removed from the area about fifteen years ago, leaving an open, grassy field around the tumuli.

I stopped to explore the Devil's Jumps, climbing to the top of one of the barrows and sitting down for another rest. I could see the rest of the mounds spread throughout the field, some large, others smaller. I was worried that it might be disrespectful to climb up and sit on a burial mound but then decided that it was okay since they had all been excavated. No signs were indicating what or what not to do, and I wasn't entirely sure what was appropriate in terms of tumulus etiquette. There probably wasn't such a thing.

There was something deeply humbling about sitting in the middle of such an ancient historical site, and I was reminded of the week's Akashic records reading:

> *"Holly, you are discovering your roots! When you travel countryside to countryside you are walking the paths of you ancestors. They each sing a song for you. Do you ever hear it? You might hear music or not...*
>
> *They are urging you to develop a love for them...to discover where they came from and the missions they served. They are asking you to help them complete their missions because of various reasons they could not. Listen in the wind. The answers lie there.*
>
> *They speak in the wind and send messages to you about this...just listen."*

I felt like there was something significant about this historical site, but I wasn't sure quite what. Sadly, I failed to receive any messages that the wind might have for me. Still, there wasn't much to do but wander around in the sun among the barrows. I felt torn between wanting to spend more time at the site and feeling like I should get back on the Way, and in the end, that's what I did. Each day involved a series of decisions: should I take a detour to a particular site, or should I head straight toward my destination that evening? It was a delicate balance of enjoying all the sights that the trail had to offer and also making sure I had enough energy to enjoy the actual walking itself by not overdoing it.

From there, the trail headed out of the woods and back into the sunshine. It continued along a fenced-in track that ran between fields and which was lined with white daisies. Off in the distance, I could see a huge field of brightly colored foxgloves, one larger than I had ever seen before. Earlier on the path, there had been large fields of them as well. This part of the Way headed over Cocking Down, and I knew I was close to my destination, but I was so tired that it just didn't feel close enough, despite the shorter walk that day.

I stopped once more to rest on a log with a view over the South Downs. I drank a bit more water, but I was acutely aware that I hadn't had enough that day, as I hadn't needed to go to the bathroom even once since I started walking. I still couldn't see the village of Cocking in the distance, so I didn't want to finish off my water just yet. I continued up a sloping hill and down the other side, so tired that I was barely trudging along.

I was once again grateful for my Pacerpoles, which helped keep me going down the track. They kept my posture in good form and helped me retain my balance on uneven trails. The poles made it much easier to walk with a steady rhythm. They were one of my top three best investments in gear on this walk, the other two being my Meindl boots and my Osprey pack.

As I descended the hill through open farmland, I walked past a massive ball of chalk, which had been placed along the South Downs Way in 2002 by artist Andy Goldsworthy in an attempt to study weathering. There had once been five chalk balls, and now there remained just one, which was not very noteworthy except that it was the one landmark that made me aware of how close I was to Cocking. I scanned the horizon and could already see the little village off in the distance.

The last bit of the Way was hot, long, and tiring. The trail was easy enough, but it was open and sunny, with no trees to shade it. I was exhausted and stressed by the fact that it had become a byway filled with giant tractors hauling a trailer. There was not enough room for both me and for the tractors, so every time I saw one, I'd have to run back to a side road and hide while it went by. I had to continually be aware of where I was in relation to my next hiding point.

After crossing paths twice with the tractors, I became motivated enough to speed walk the rest of the way to the turnoff to Cocking. Unfortunately, in my haste to escape the tractors, I forgot that my guidebook indicated a quick turnoff near a water tap, which led down a tree-lined track to the village. Before I reached the water tap, I saw a footpath sign that indicated just 3/4 miles to Cocking, so I took that trail. It was narrow, overgrown, and lined with tall hedges, making it difficult to walk with my poles, but it was shady, which was most welcome after such a hot, sunny day.

The path headed steeply downhill and out onto a street, which wound around through a small residential area of cottages before I ended up on Cocking's main road. The first thing I saw was a sign indicating just 50 meters to Moonlight Cottage, my B&B. I was thrilled. I was even more excited when I saw how cute the inside of the cottage was, and when I was told that I was the only guest that evening, which was unexpected. I looked forward to peace and solitude after a tiring day, though I had enjoyed my time at the farmhouse with the others.

The Evening

My feet were aching, and so was the rest of me. By now, I did not find this to be surprising. After a quick shower in the shared bathroom—which of course I was sharing with no one that night—I washed my clothes, wrung them out well, hung them up in the window of my room to begin the first stage of the drying process, and then plopped down on the bed to investigate my guidebook. It looked like Cocking had a small village store, so I headed straight there to stock up on bottled water. I had made one quick pit stop just before I reached the last leg of the Way with the tractors, and I was aware that I hadn't had enough water that day. I planned to get a bigger bottle or perhaps an extra one for the following day.

Cocking was such a tiny village that it appeared I could walk from one end to the next in under three minutes. It seemed like its sole means of existence was to provide lodging for South Downs walkers: it was dotted throughout with cottages, B&Bs, and the only services appeared to be the lone pub and the tiny village store, for which I was grateful. I stocked up on water and bought a bag of crisps, and the store-keeper warned me that it was due to be even hotter the following day. Despite this, I mistakenly reasoned that just one extra bottle would be enough, though there would be no water taps along the next stage of the Way.

There was a lone tap right where the trail from Cocking met up with the South Downs Way, which seemed absurd since Cocking was a common place for people to stay. Surely it would make more sense to have a water tap halfway in the middle of a stage, rather than at the start or the end of one. However, it appeared that the few water taps that existed along the Way had more to do with where it was convenient to install one, rather than where one might be convenient for walkers.

From the village store, I headed straight to the B&B's pretty, flower-filled garden to drink a cold bottle of sparkling water, eat my bag of crisps, and review the day's events. I was starving after having eaten only the small sandwich for lunch, but I had to wait until at least six when the lone pub of Cocking opened. Despite my fatigue, this part of the Way had been well sign-posted. This was the first day that I hadn't gotten lost at all, which had made the walk much more straightforward. Either that or I had learned my lesson and was now paying more attention to the signposts.

As I was typing out my day's experience on my iPad, Maggie and Martin, the couple I had met at the farm, passed by on the little road behind the B&B's garden. I stood up to greet them and to ask how their day had gone. It had taken them two full hours longer than it had taken me to walk this stretch of the

Way. It was clear that they had opted for a leisurely walk, taking photographs as they went along, and I was back to speed walking as usual—in as much as I could. Plus, they had taken the long way around Beacon Hill and then gotten lost a bit, whereas I had taken the not so "fun" trail straight up and over the top.

Finally, six o'clock came around, and I walked down the street to the pub, which was happily quiet and empty, as it had just opened minutes before. I chose a table and ordered a burger and fries. I had considered ordering something light and healthy like fish but was so hungry that I felt like I needed something meatier and more substantial—something more *grounding*. I settled in with my dinner and a half-pint of beer. Maggie and Martin walked in and settled down two tables down from me.

When I finished my meal, I went over to discuss the day's walk with them. After hearing tales of people walking the Camino de Santiago and meeting people along the way, I finally understood how nice it was to cross paths with the same people every day, even if it was just for a quick chat. It was these brief moments of social activity that complemented my solitary experience on the South Downs each day.

After exiting the pub, I planned to head back to my B&B but instead decided to take a quick detour off the main street to the St. Catherine of Siena Church, the oldest parts of which date back to the 11th century. The church is a Grade I Listed building, which means that it has been placed on the Statutory List of Buildings of Special Architectural or Historic Interest. A Grade I designation means that it is considered a building of exceptional interest, which in this case, includes remnants of a 13th-century wall painting.

After walking through the churchyard and taking some photos, I tried the door, but it was locked, as so many village churches are during the week. I was disappointed, but also tired and eager to return to my B&B, so I walked out of the churchyard and down the street to my B&B, where I settled into my room, first reading and then listening to music on my phone as I relaxed. My room had a small window, which I had opened as wide as I could, to let the breeze in at night and to dry my clothes. It wasn't long before I turned the lights out and went to sleep.

DAY 4

COCKING TO AMBERLEY: 12+3 MILES (19+4.8 KM)

Valerian–Delight in the Moment was this day's theme. This day's oracle card sounded pretty exciting to me —dare I say "delightful"—and I was looking forward to the day's walk, though I was already feeling a bit disappointed that after this day, the journey would be halfway over. I resolved to enjoy each moment of the day's walk, and each subsequent day on the trail.

The Morning

Moonlight Cottage had the best shower and the best bed so far, and I slept perfectly throughout the night. I was so exhausted by 10 pm that I had to put my iPad to charge and go to bed. I tried to listen to a new guided meditation that I had recently downloaded from Aurora, channeled by my friend Cara Wilde, but I fell asleep for most of it. I remembered waking up twice during the meditation and thinking, "oh yes, this is that new meditation I was listening to" before falling instantly asleep again.

Once again, I woke up just before 6 am but lay in bed for a

while. Because of something I had read the night before, I was no longer surprised by my early rising. I generally don't wake up until 8 am or later, even on a workday, as I'm not a morning person. And because I'm self-employed, I can plan my days however I want, starting and finishing a bit later than most people. But I had been reading Robert Twigger's book *Walk*, and in it, he says that on long-distance walks, he noticed he requires less actual sleep, even getting as little as five and a half hours a night.

Time spent in a horizontal position can be as regenerating as time spent sleeping, as I read in *Walk*. I was still sleeping almost seven hours a night, but my hours had shifted earlier, which was perfect for walking. I had ordered my breakfast for 7:30 am because I was hoping to be on the trail a bit earlier than on the three previous days. Moonlight Cottage was the most organized of all B&Bs thus far and had presented me with a form upon arrival to request what I wanted for breakfast and also for a sack lunch. I was impressed with their efficiency.

After three days on the Way, I had moments where I felt as though I could stay in this world forever: the world of endless Nature. There was an abundance of trails to choose from should I ever decide to stray from the South Downs Way, and a collection of gorgeous little English villages just off the main path for accommodation each night. Life was so pleasantly simple. All I had to do was put one foot in front of the other until I arrived at my destination. Everything I needed was in my backpack—food, clothing—and I would find shelter at each day's B&B.

This feeling of being in a different world—a beautiful, simple one—was so strong that I was shocked to see a road sign in Cocking that indicated the way to Guildford, a city just twelve miles from where I lived. That seemed so close to home, and yet I felt so far away from it. So far, all of the villages I had stayed in were inaccessible by train. While they were, of course, easily accessible by car, they somehow felt as though I would only ever be able to reach them by walking the Downs, should I ever want to revisit them. Arriving by car would feel like sacrilege.

On this day's walk, I was determined to drink more water. The previous night, I had filled up an extra small bottle of water and placed it next to my pack. This day was yet another one without water taps. And if it was supposed to be even hotter this day than it had been the day before, I needed to be extra careful.

I also resolved to take it easier. I was back to a slightly longer thirteen-mile walk, which meant that this stage was two miles longer than the previous day. I was feeling a bit disappointed that I had allowed my fatigue to rule my decisions the previous day, as I would have liked to explore the burial grounds at the Devil's Jumps a little bit longer. But no worry—I could always return.

Perhaps on this day, when I meant to Delight in the Moment, I would find the balance between my energy levels and my desire to explore the treasures of the South Downs. Maybe the secret was just to take more breaks, no matter what time I arrived at my destination. I had told most of the B&Bs that I would be arriving after 4 pm, so there was no reason to rush, even if I was feeling tired and achy—or perhaps *especially* since I was feeling tired and achy.

What I didn't know at this point in the morning was that Day 4 was to be the hardest day yet. Later that afternoon, I would trudge awkwardly into Amberley and then despair that I still had a mere three blocks to walk before arriving at my B&B. I would end up sitting down on a bench less than two blocks from the B&B because I needed one final rest. Today would be the day of most rest stops. It would also be the hottest, sunniest day thus far if you can imagine that.

The Walk

This stage of the walk, twelve miles from Cocking to Amberley, follows a chalk lane through farms before it reaches Heyshott Down, then follows the edge of woodland before passing Graffham Down on one side and Bronze Age tumuli (burial mounds) on the other. From here, it heads into Roman territory, passing through part of Stane Street, the old Roman road from London to Chichester. At this point, there's a detour off the Way down to the Bignor Roman Villa, the home of surprisingly well-preserved Roman mosaics. The Way on this stage is relatively open as it runs through farmland on its way down to Amberley, which marks the halfway point on the trail.

The sky was a deep blue, fading off at the edges. I didn't know it at this point, but there would not be a single cloud in the sky for the entire day. I departed Moonlight Cottage earlier than usual, having had my breakfast right on time at 7:30 am. I made another quick trip to the corner store to get tissues, and I ended up walking out with hay fever eye drops and hay fever one-a-day pills as well. I had spent the morning blowing my nose, and I didn't want problems on the trail, which was full of grasses and grain. I was stocked up and ready to go.

I decided to take the official trail back up to the Way, as designated in my guidebook, thinking for some reason that it might be less steep. This thinking was, of course, ridiculous, as the only way back up to the South Downs Way was uphill. The trail wound around and then headed steadily upwards. It continued that way for so long that once again, I feared I might be on the wrong track: I could vaguely hear the main road off to the right, but it seemed to be too far away.

It made me wonder: at what point do we commit to the path that we're on? I considered turning back to Cocking and taking the same trail I had used the previous day, but despaired at having to backtrack downhill to then scale a similar hill to the one I was on once more. It made more sense to continue for a few minutes and see where I would come out on this path.

Eventually, I made it to the connection with the South Downs Way, and there I found the water tap. I had brought one extra water bottle, for a total of almost two liters, but I was tempted to drink some of my water already so that I could take advantage of the tap and fill up. At the time, I thought I'd be okay with two liters of water in that heat. Now, in retrospect, I realize just how much I had dangerously underestimated my hydration needs. This poor planning would end up adding an unexpected detour to this day's walking, but I didn't know that just yet.

My right heel was bothering me a bit, but I refused to look at it. I was confident that if I hadn't gotten blisters thus far, then I was safe. After all, it was Day 4! I had bought a great pair of boots and had worn them in for over 100 miles before starting the Way, as was recommended to break in new shoes before a long journey.

My socks were clean and dry each day, and I followed the advice of applying a thin coat of Vaseline to my feet each morning before putting my socks on. I would later realize that in this heat, I would have been better off merely letting my feet air out during lunch breaks and changing socks halfway through the day so that my feet would have dry socks to walk in. But this was a lesson I had not yet learned.

The trail headed steadily uphill in the blazing sun, through a farm that had an excellent series of signs explaining all about their livestock. There was a sign next to the chicken coop indicating which breeds of chickens they had, and what color eggs each one laid. Further on, there was a sign that explained the different breeds of sheep they had in the fields. I stopped to read each sign, delighting in the moment. I loved learning more about the farms I was passing on the South Downs.

Exiting the farm, the Way continued along the edge of a

deeply wooded forest, which offered its shade to the trail. It was hot already, but for the first third of today's walk, the trail alternated between open farmlands with scorching sun and more cooling woodland paths. The shady woods continued, with the bonus of a collection of Bronze Age tumuli just alongside the trail, on both sides of it. I was debating about whether to take a detour to the Roman villa in Bignor. According to my guidebook it was just 25 minutes off the Way, which probably meant an hour and a half detour in total. It was tempting, but I wasn't sure I wanted to add to the twelve miles I had planned for this stage of the walk.

The path emerged from the woodland into an open field of grain, sloping gradually downhill. The trail cut straight through the field, with views of the South Downs every which way. I was starting to feel the heat even more now that I was back out in the sun. I was beginning to think the detour to the Roman villa would be compulsory so that I could refill my water supply, as my guidebook indicated it had a tea room with refreshments.

The farms in this area had a series of educational signs on each fence, detailing different aspects of the work that they did, including how hedgerows are made and how to tell the difference between wheat, barley, and oats in the fields. I stopped to read them all, reminding myself to take my time and delight in the moment. At the base of the field, the trail came out onto a road, and I crossed into another farm. I walked for a few minutes until I found a tree where I could take a break under its shade. I studied the maps for this day's walk, reviewing the landmarks to see exactly where I was so I could mentally ration my water, splitting up my remaining amount into stages.

The path began to climb steadily through fields, with a line of trees alongside it that somehow failed to shade the trail. I regularly stopped to sip my water. I had finally mastered the ability to contort my right arm around to where my smaller bottle was located so I could drink without taking off my pack.

There was little water left, and a detour to the Roman villa was looking more and more to be a sure thing.

I calculated roughly at what point in the day I would arrive at the Roman villa (according to me, about 1 pm). I decided to eat my lunch at 12:30, about five hours after breakfast, and supposedly at the point where I departed the South Downs Way for the Roman villa. Shortly before entering the National Trust property of the Slindon Estate, I found one shady tree to have lunch underneath.

I'd seen so few people this day, even fewer than on the previous day. The group of six runners I had seen near Beacon Hill the previous day passed me by, once more with no hats on their heads. Most of them weren't carrying water, either. They had managed to survive the previous day's run, but today seemed even hotter, and I was amazed at how well they appeared to be doing. These men were truly impressive.

I was already tired, and I knew the heat wasn't helping. After I finished my lunch, I stood up, grunting and groaning as I slowly got to my feet and heaved my pack onto my back. My moans turned to laughter as I looked up to see a couple just steps from where I was standing. I realized that I had gotten so used to being alone for hours at a time that my level of personal sound effects had increased. I would never have made all that noise if I had seen those two people on the trail before I got up.

Being alone is something that I enjoy, and I was in my element out here alone on the trail. I loved walking alone, even though I was increasingly concerned about my water supply. I stopped once more to sit on a bench and rest, taking a sip of water. I knew for sure at this point that I would be heading down to the Roman villa to refill my water supply. It was a simple detour that was sure to solve my problem, but I was obsessing about my low water supplies much more than I needed to. You would think I was hiking through the desert.

I entered the Slindon Estate and walked past fields of sheep, grazing out in the open sun. The Slindon Estate is a 3,500 acre agricultural and woodland estate on the South Downs, which is managed by the National Trust, which has owned the estate since 1950. The Roman road of Stane Street, which crosses the Downs here as it makes its way to London from Chichester, and no doubt is the reason that the villa in Bignor lies so close to the South Downs Way and the Slindon Estate.

By this time, it had been quite a while since I had seen a genuinely shady stretch of trail. I knew I was close to the turnoff for the Roman villa at Bignor, as I came upon a sign in Latin indicating the directions to Londinium (London) and Noviomagus (Chichester, apparently). This part of the South Downs Way ran along part of Stane Street, the old Roman road stretching from London Bridge to the Roman town of Noviomagus Reginorum, which was later renamed Chichester by the Saxons. I was looking forward to arriving at Bignor to relax and refill my water and to have a cup of tea.

The road to the villa was well signposted, and I headed down a deliciously shaded road, with not a car in sight. There was a thick plantation of trees all along the way, and they provided much-needed shelter from the sunshine. I came out of the shaded road into open farmland, walking past a barn and following the clear signs to the villa, which was the only tourist destination in the area. The walk took more than 25 minutes and looked like it would be more like 45 by the time I arrived at my destination. I saw another turnoff for the villa and realized it was a full tourist complex, as two huge tour buses were parked in its grassy lot. It seemed to take forever to get to the actual buildings, but there was no wait at all to get my ticket and head inside into the refreshingly cool shade of the building.

Now that I was here, I was going to delight in the moment and enjoy the museum. The mosaics were beautiful and remarkably well preserved; it was awe-inspiring to think that they had survived for so many years. A farmer had discovered the site as recently as 1811, as he was plowing his field, and just three years later, the site opened as a tourist attraction. The villa is thought to date back to the 3rd century AD, though there is evidence that a farmstead was located on this site as early as the 1st century AD. The villa was extended over the years, and in its final phase—finished between 300 and 350 AD—it had over sixty-five rooms, plus farm buildings. The mosaics are in excellent condition, and it is thought they were installed during the final stage of expansion. The museum has laid them out as they were found, with the museum buildings raised around them to protect the tiles.

After carefully navigating around the many schoolchildren who were also visiting, I made it out to the teashop and ordered four bottles of water: three still and one sparkling. I sat on a bench for a few minutes, intending to drink the bottle of sparkling, but I saw that it was a quarter past two, and I realized that it might be best to get back to the trail. I had delighted in the moment while enjoying the mosaics, but I was eager to get back to the Way, as I still had five miles to go to get to Amberley, the day's final destination. And so I decided: no tea for me.

In the end, Bignor villa turned out to be about a 45-minute walk back to the Way, where I arrived at just past three, precisely two hours after I had started my detour. The trek back up was grueling, as the road was quite steep, and somehow it wasn't as shady as I had remembered it being just two hours earlier. In a ridiculous attempt to make things easier on myself —to be honest, I have no idea what I was thinking—I tried walking backward for a bit, but I wasn't sure whether that made the steep climb easier or more difficult. At least it used different muscles, which was kind of restful.

Eventually, I arrived at the top of the hill. Grateful to be back out on the Way, I headed steadily upwards once again in the scorching sun between fields of grain. This time, I was

confident that I had more than enough water to reach Amberley, which was one less thing to worry about. I had finished one
bottle on the hill back up to the Way, but I still had three more.
I may be tired, but I would surely be well hydrated!

My guidebook encouraged walkers to look out for Roman
coins in the dust, and I did. However, it appeared highly
unlikely that I would come across any so many years after
Roman occupation and on such a highly transited trail. Plus, I
was walking at such a steady pace that it seemed silly to even
think about finding any coins. Still, it gave me something to do
as I walked—as if walking alone weren't enough—and the
thought of finding a long lost Roman coin seemed exciting.

I was no longer concerned about walking too fast, and
missing things: the heat made it impossible to walk at my usual
brisk pace. Instead, I plodded slowly along, enjoying the
gorgeous views along the top of the Downs. The expansive
views across golden fields and rolling hills were something I
thought I would never tire of. Eventually, the trail shifted to a
downhill slope, running at times between shrubs that
somehow did not manage to shade the path at all.

I was more tired than I had been all week, and every time I
stopped to take a break, I desperately brought out my guidebook so I could estimate the remaining time of my walk to
Amberley. I was struggling to delight in the moment of the
journey when I so badly wanted to reach my destination for
that evening. It looked like I would arrive between five and six
in the afternoon, though I desperately hoped it would be
sooner. It was at this point that I recalled my theme for the day,
Delight in the Moment, and began to use it as a mantra,
repeating it over and over again out loud.

It seemed to help, so I turned it into a song, walking down
the path singing different versions of a not very original song
whose only lyrics were "delight in the moment." Surprisingly,
there were many different ways I could sing that one phrase. I

couldn't seem to manage more creativity than that, but the rhythm kept me going and helped me to focus on something other than my tiredness. I vowed to enjoy the views as I sang to myself.

The Way wound around and back up another hill, also devoid of trees or shade, as it once again cut through fields of grain. I continued to sip water at regular intervals, stopping to sit and have a drink of water whenever I came across a lone tree that provided a bit of shade. The path continued steadily down until it was finally engulfed in the shade of numerous trees.

I settled down in the grass alongside the trail and had a drink of water, then pulled out my guidebook once again to review the path ahead. It was past 4pm, and I estimated that I might actually make it to Amberley by five. I turned off the airplane mode on my phone to see if I had any signal. To my surprise, I did, so I texted Agustín and posted a few of the Instagram photos I had taken during the day. I still felt very far from my destination that day, but also lucky to have a bit of an internet connection, as I knew I would arrive later than usual, and I didn't want anyone to worry.

I came out of the shade and crossed a busy road to once again enter more farmland, this time with a view of three small bits of the village. I searched the horizon for Amberley castle, which was the only landmark I knew would be evident from this distance. The castle was initially built as a 12th-century manor house and was fortified in 1377, then used as a fortress by the bishops of Chichester until the death of Bishop Robert Sherborne, who died in 1536. A string of several tenants later leased the castle before it was eventually sold to a private family. It was used as a hunting lodge for many years and was subsequently sold over and over again, passing through the hands of different owners during the 20th century before it was bought in 2014 by the current owners. It now operates as a hotel and restaurant.

I could see a castle far out, at the most remote of the villages, but because it was so far away, I hoped it was Arundel castle instead. Arundel is a larger town situated relatively close to Amberley that also has a large castle. However, I knew from a previous walk I had done in the area that the castle I could see was most likely Amberley's. I paused to take a break to consult my guidebook once again. The castle appeared to be Amberley's if I was reading the maps right. The trail, however, reached the village by a very indirect route. It first wound around, crossed a bridge over the River Arun, crossed another bridge over the train line (the first train tracks I had seen in four days), and took what seemed the most extensive loop ever to get to the village of Amberley. I took at least two more breaks before I reached Amberley.

Once I entered the village, I pulled out the directions to my B&B and despaired a bit at having to walk just three more blocks to reach it—I was ridiculously tired. I saw a bench at the side of the road and headed toward it, plopping myself down for yet another rest. After a few minutes, I dragged myself up and headed toward that night's accommodation. I could barely lift my feet by the time I walked into the garden. I was so grateful to have made it to my final destination for that day, having continued the Delight in the Moment song on and off for the last two hours of my walk in a desperate attempt to keep my spirits up. In the end, I walked into my B&B at twenty to six, almost two hours after I had initially estimated my arrival would be. It had been a long day's walk.

The Evening

My B&B hosts were delightful; their home was one of the best of my whole journey along the South Downs Way. The owner was outside in the garden and heard me walk up to the house, and she guided me around through the garden, where I took my boots off before entering. She showed me to my room and my private bathroom and then offered me tea and cake.

After such a long, hot day, the prospect of tea and cake seemed impossibly perfect, especially since I had left the Roman villa before enjoying a cup of tea that afternoon. I sat outside in the beautifully designed garden, enjoying tea and homemade strawberry shortcake, which was baked earlier that day. The garden was filled with different colored flowers everywhere I looked and was a shady, relaxing haven after a long day's walk. I was so grateful to have arrived in one piece and to have a place to sit down in the cool shade. It also provided me with a chance to rest a bit before heading into the shower. As always, I felt like my dirty, stinky presence was out of place in my clean B&B, which in this case was the nicest I had stayed in thus far and would turn out to be the best place I stayed the entire journey. I was looking forward to cleaning up.

I relished my refreshing shower, and as I dressed afterward, I was horrified to discover several unpleasant things had appeared on my body. I had blisters on my feet, a bizarre rash covering my legs, insect bites everywhere, and sunburn on one arm—yes, just one arm. It was so much to discover, all at once. My body was an absolute mess, and everything ached. I felt like the battle wounds had finally begun to show from the walk. I wasn't surprised; after all, I felt like I had barely made it to my destination that afternoon.

Looking at the blisters, rash, bites, and burn, I realized just how challenging the day had been. I was anxious to see whether the rash improved the following day, and I wondered just how much my blisters would dry up overnight. The sunburn was sure to be better by morning, and luckily the insect bites didn't itch. But I was aware of just how stressful the day had been, and my body bore the marks to prove it.

These battle scars from the day's walk got me nervous about the rest of my journey: I had already made it exactly halfway to

Eastbourne, fifty miles. But the days had been more or less evenly spread out, despite having extended the days for one reason or another. The second half of my journey would not be as smooth: Day 5 was a manageable thirteen miles, Day 6 was a horrifying 20 miles, and Day 7 was again thirteen miles. The final day was a leisurely eleven miles, albeit with lots of ups and downs over the Seven Sisters, a series of sloping chalk cliffs on the coast.

I recalculated and realized it would be much more manageable to add an extra day to my journey and split Day 6 into two. The thought of attempting 20 miles in one day, a plan that had once seemed reasonable, now terrified me. I studied the maps in my guidebook and found the two villages that could replace Lewes as a stop. I had been fantasizing about changing my route all through the day, and when I arrived in Amberley after just fifteen miles, it was clear to me that it would have been impossible to walk an extra five that day. A 20-mile day was just too much for me at this point.

The B&B owner drove me to a nearby pub for dinner, and once I was seated and had ordered, I desperately began to phone B&Bs in the first village. There were three options, and only one of them answered the phone to tell me there was no vacancy on the night I needed it. I anxiously continued to dial the other two B&Bs, eventually realizing that it would be next to impossible to rearrange my itinerary on such short notice, so I turned to my phone to check the weather forecast.

It was due to rain on Thursday, so with fingers crossed for good luck with the weather (for once, I was hoping that it actually *would* rain for my walk), I resolved to brave the twenty miles from Bramber to Lewes on Day 6. I knew that part of what made my days so tricky was the heat, and rain would cool everything off. I convinced myself that a rainy day would make my twenty-mile walk feasible. And so, I resolved to quit worrying and continue with my original plan.

After deciding that I would indeed be able to complete the rest of my journey, my confidence wore down once again when I got up from the pub a leisurely two hours later for the short walk back to my B&B. I had only had sparkling water with dinner and chamomile tea afterward, but I must have looked utterly drunk from the way I was walking. Everything ached from the waist down, and I hobbled along awkwardly back to my B&B. It was just a ten-minute walk, but I was practically counting the steps back to my bed. If I hadn't been in such pain, I would have giggled at myself the entire way.

DAY 5

AMBERLEY TO BRAMBER: 13 MILES (21 KM)

P lantain–Regeneration was the theme for the day. I had consulted my list of daily themes before going to bed the night before, and I had been hoping that this day's theme would come true: the previous day had left me with blisters on my feet, a rash on my legs, insect bites, and sunburn on one arm, and I went to bed feeling optimistic that it would all be resolved by morning.

The Morning

Unfortunately, I was unable to get a good night's rest. My room had large windows, and while I had left them all open during the night, unfortunately, it wasn't enough to keep me cool while I slept. There was no night breeze, and it hadn't cooled off much from the afternoon. I tossed and turned, feeling hot and sticky in bed.

In the morning, I woke to a symphony of birds at 4 am, and shortly after that, my hay fever kicked in, which kept me up for almost an hour. I took my one-a-day hay fever pills and returned to bed, armed with a handful of tissues, and determined to remain in a horizontal position. I was eventually able to get back to sleep, waking only when my alarm went off. I probably could have slept in even more, but I had ordered my breakfast for 7:30 once again, hoping to get an early start on the trail.

I was mostly feeling regenerated. The blisters had drained and dried, which was good. My legs were still covered in the rash, but it didn't hurt or itch, so I decided to ignore it. The insect bites weren't much of a bother, and the sunburn had mostly turned to tan. All in all, things had improved overnight. Regeneration!

My B&B host cooked me what I can only describe as the most magnificent full English breakfast I had ever been served, with the addition of plain yogurt and fresh berries. It was delicious, but I was unable to finish it all, and I was eager to get out on the trail. I was sad to leave this gorgeous floral haven, the best B&B I had stayed in so far, and, I would later realize, the best accommodation on the entire trip. After breakfast, I pulled my pack onto my shoulders, put my boots on in the garden, and headed out of Amberley village, clicking down the road with my Pacerpoles to return to the South Downs Way.

The Walk

The thirteen miles from Amberley to Bramber start as a leisurely walk along the high crest of the South Downs, with great views. At one point, the Way crosses the busy A24 road before heading up to Chanctonbury Ring, a circle of beech trees planted in 1760 on the site of an Iron Age hillfort. From there, the Way winds through farmland down into the twin villages of Bramber and Upper Beeding, which sit on either side of the River Adur.

As usual, I started on the trail feeling rested, refreshed, and ready to go, this time with my earliest start yet: about a quarter past eight. I was, however, eager to get back on the Way and so I avoided making a quick detour to Amberley's 12th-century church, which dates back to around the year 1100. I had learned from previous days that it was best to avoid detours.

For the same reason, I had brought an extra bottle of water with me. My water supply seemed to be increasing every day, and I wondered how much water I would end up carting around by the final day of my walk. My only consolation was that the more water I drank, the more I lightened my load.

As was the case most mornings, I was feeling optimistic about this day's walk, and my stomach fluttered with excitement when I spotted the sign leading back onto the Way. I was about to re-enter that magical world of the South Downs. After walking down the busy B2139 road to get back on the Way, the path headed uphill as it did every morning. Each day, I headed down off the trail into a village where I would spend the night, and the following morning meant climbing back up another hill to get started once again. The sloping uphill trail quickly turned into a steeper grade as the South Downs Way headed up a second hill.

The trail continued straight on across the Downs ridge, with views to both sides. Once again, I could see the coast off to the right, a hazy stripe of gray-blue water off in the distance. Despite predictions of this being the hottest day yet (it seemed that each day's weather prediction was to be hotter than the previous one), it felt much cooler than the day before. The sky was a bit overcast, and there was a refreshing breeze that cooled things off even more. The few clouds in the sky were my friends.

After some time on the trail, I realized that I wasn't feeling very Regenerated. My aches and pains were gone, but the blistery bits of my feet did not feel that great, and Compeed wasn't always a magic solution.

Compeed is a European brand of gel bandages for treating

blisters, and was originally developed in Denmark. It's applied directly on top of the blister, where it somehow absorbs the blister liquid (assuming you haven't already drained the blister yourself), eventually turning into a soft mass that cushions the blister. It also seals the blister, forming a sort of cushioned "second skin" and allowing new skin to grow underneath the bandage. This little gel cushion relieves pain by protecting the blister from rubbing directly against your socks. It repels water, and stops dirt and germs from entering the blister, thus preventing infection, which is always a good thing! You're meant to stick it directly on top of the blister, and let it remain there until it falls off, usually a few days later.

I'm aware that this sounds like an advertisement for Compeed, but this stuff is truly amazing. It's a vital part of any hiker's first aid kit, and I always buy them in a variety of sizes. Compeed comes in little plastic cases that you can easily slip into your pack. While it's much more expensive than the average bandage, it's also much more effective in treating blisters than the ordinary bandage.

After I had been walking for about a mile, I stopped in the shade to remove my boot and sock to inspect my heel. It felt like the Compeed had come off my heel; it wasn't cushioning the blister at all. To my surprise, there it was, glued snugly to my foot. For some reason, it wasn't doing its job in cushioning the blister and stopping the pain like it usually did.

My daily theme mantra began much earlier today: I turned "Regeneration" into a song and started singing it over and over, whenever I felt frustrated with my feet. The weather was perfect; the only problem was the pain in my feet. Both my right heel and my left little toe hurt.

I continued for another mile, hobbling slowly along the trail and feeling like I had a stone between my heel and my boot. I fantasized about having an extra pair of shoes to wear, like my Vibram Fivefingers that I often wore for hiking and which I had neglected to bring with me, in the interest of packing light. I wanted anything on my feet but my hot boots, which meant that my fantasies now turned to Birkenstocks, my evening shoes.

My thinking was that they would be cool, breezy, and comfortable, but they'd also fill up with dust and dirt and gravel, and I'd have to shake them out regularly. Or would I? The only way to know would be to try, so after two miles of hobbling painfully in my boots, I stopped alongside the trail and took them off, peeling my socks off and dumping everything next to me. I pulled out my Birkenstock Gizehs and put them on my feet. I probably wouldn't last very long with them on my feet, but at least they'd give me a break from the boots, which I stuffed into the top of my backpack. They barely fit inside on top of everything else.

The Birks were fantastic: my feet felt cool, refreshed, and pain-free. It was like heaven on my feet. That was my best executive decision that day, and I suspected that perhaps this was what Regeneration was all about. These shoes would give my feet much needed rest from the stifling hot boots that had been giving me blisters and allow them to heal out in the open air.

I was able to pick up my pace a bit, which was good because I had been ambling along so slowly I was afraid I'd never reach my destination that evening. After I had arrived so late the previous afternoon, I was seriously concerned about reaching Bramber before it got too close to dusk. I had started my South Downs journey worried about walking too fast, and now I was concerned that I was walking too slowly. The difference between day walking and long-distance walking was becoming painfully clear to me.

But the important thing was that I was no longer in pain, and I hiked happily down the hill toward the water tap at Washington, where I filled up my bottles to replace what I had already consumed that morning. From there, it was across the

A24 road and then back up another hill toward Chanctonbury Ring, one of the landmarks on my map. I had returned to taking numerous breaks, each time studying my map to estimate my time of arrival in Bramber.

I soon realized that I was taking much longer to walk each stretch of the trail than the book estimated. My guidebook included ranges of time for each stage of the journey, and I was now exceeding the longest estimated times between points, which meant I had absolutely no idea when I'd arrive in Bramber. My first estimate (clearly an optimistic one) was 1:30 pm. Then I extended that to 2 pm, then three, and finally decided I would arrive sometime between three and four.

People were passing me whenever they came up behind me on the trail, something I had never experienced before. I had always been the one to pass other people when walking. A couple passed me while I was eating my lunch alongside the path just before reaching Chanctonbury Ring, and by the time I got up just a few minutes later, they were so far along down the way I couldn't even see them. I remembered the wish I had had at the start of my journey to slow down and enjoy the trail. It seemed that my body was forcing me to make this wish a reality. I supposed I should be careful about what I hoped for.

I had also incorrectly estimated how to arrive at Bramber. There was a small group of three villages that were very close to one another: Steyning, Upper Beeding, and Bramber. I had thought I would approach the village via Steyning, as my guidebook showed a clear path toward Steyning. This route might have allowed me to arrive a bit earlier. Still, once I saw that further along the trail there was a specific turnoff for Bramber, I realized I'd have to continue much farther than I had initially estimated. Sometimes, it just wasn't clear where to turn off the South Downs Way to get to my accommodation at night.

I stopped once more just on the outer edge of Chanctonbury Ring, enjoying a bit of shade while I sipped my water. An entire flock of sheep seemed to have the same idea as I had, and it was challenging to find a bit of ground that was free of sheep pellets. Still, the shade was very, very welcome. Another couple sat far off to my left, enjoying their lunch. The Ring was easily accessible from a car park I had passed just before heading up the hill, so it was a popular spot for day walkers, even though it was a weekday.

Chanctonbury Ring is a circle of beech trees sitting atop Chanctonbury Hill, which was originally a small hill fort dating back to the early Iron Age, in the 6th to 5th centuries BCE. However, Bronze Age pottery has also been found on the site, indicating that it may be even older than initially estimated. After the hillfort was abandoned, the Romans used it as a religious site and built two temples on the hill. Chanctonbury Hill is no longer famous for its history as a hill fort, but rather for the circle of trees, which were planted in 1760 by Charles Goring.

Local legend has it that the ring of trees was planted not by Goring but rather by the devil, who can be summoned by running around the circle seven times in a counter-clockwise direction (it's a relatively large circle of trees, so this will also give you a good workout). Once the devil appears, he will offer you a bowl of soup in exchange for your soul, which quite frankly doesn't seem like an equal exchange. Other legends state that women who sleep just one night underneath the trees will experience increased fertility, which (if that's what you're looking for) sounds like a better deal than the devil's soup. It also involves less running.

Not wanting to waste too much time resting, I stood up to continue on my journey, heading out from under the shade of the Ring and back into open, grassy fields. My Birkenstocks were still going strong, and they were not getting too many stones stuck in them. It was indeed a South Downs miracle. I didn't have to stop more than once an hour to shake out a pebble. These sandals had saved the day. Granted, after pausing to slather sunblock on my feet, they had acquired a thin coat of dust on top and looked as though they had been sprinkled with cocoa powder, but that would be easy enough to clean off in the shower. The dirt was a welcome alternative to the hot, blistered feet I had experienced just that morning.

I was passing landmark after landmark on my map, stopping at least once an hour to sit down and recoup my energy. I could see the sea off to the right once again, and I knew I was close to Bramber, which made me feel antsy to arrive. Once again, I focused on the destination, not the journey itself—which was the whole reason I was there! I realized that — despite my regular mantra singing of the day's theme, Regeneration—I still wasn't feeling very regenerated, nor was I enjoying the walk very much that day. It was just okay, and I was no longer walking in the present moment as I had been for most of the previous days: I was focused solely on arriving in Bramber, and I was once again worried about my 20-mile walk the following day to Lewes. With my newly acquired blisters, I could barely walk thirteen miles in one day; how was I going to manage?

By that point, I was even entertaining the idea of giving up at some point and just going home. Maybe I just wasn't cut out to complete a long-distance trail. The only problem was that most of the villages I was staying in had no rail stations, and getting home from any of the locations would be tricky. I was reasonably close to home, and yet it still felt like I was in a whole different world.

It soon became apparent that my Birkenstocks trick was only going to work for one day: it was still due to rain the next day, and besides, they were starting to rub between my toes on my left foot. I realized that I was simply trading one set of blisters for another, however fantastic it might have felt today. The trail was beginning to slope down, and I saw the turnoff I was initially planning to take toward Steyning. I was tempted just to take it, but was afraid of it turning out to be even longer than the official turnoff. I didn't want to risk it.

The trail was a narrow dirt track between soft grassy bits, and I decided to take off my shoes altogether, picking my way carefully along in the grass in bare feet. It was soft, and it alleviated the pain between my toes. It did, however, mean that I had to walk even more slowly, as I didn't want to step on a hidden rock and mess my feet up even more. After a few minutes of padding along the grassy trail, the Birks went back on.

Shortly after, I came across a man I had seen every day on the trail since Cocking. We initially met as I was heading out the door from my B&B at Moonlight Cottage, and then I had seen him the following day near the Roman villa. He had spent the night in Bignor, near the villa, a full five miles before Amberley (plus that grueling hike up the road to get back on the Way), and he was headed for the same destination as I was. His arrival was yet another indication of my snail-paced speed on the trail. We spoke for a couple of minutes, and then he sped on alone, probably at a rate similar to how I used to walk before the South Downs. I felt like an inexperienced slowpoke and envied his speedy walking pace. Comparisonitis set in: he was a better walker than I.

Here the path continued across wide, open fields. To the left, I could see a village off in the distance. The trail began to slope down toward the tiny village of Botolphs, becoming more shaded as it did. It turned left, then right, and followed a quiet country lane past a handful of cottages.

There was a confusing left turn that wasn't sign marked, but it seemed to be the right way according to my map. I was now getting increasingly frustrated that I hadn't yet arrived at my destination. The path turned again, and I knew I was getting closer to the Bramber turnoff, but when I arrived at the place where I thought I needed to turn, it all looked different from the map—which, by the way, has been updated and improved in the most recent edition of the guidebook.

In one of my more difficult moments along the Way, I had a meltdown and cried. I just wanted to arrive at my hotel. I didn't want to walk anymore. I wanted my shower and my bed. This meltdown was, thankfully, the lowest point of my journey. I stood a little bit off the main trail, hidden among some trees, and I pouted and sniffled alongside the path like a small child, and somehow it made me feel a bit better. I was ready to go once again. All of my pent up frustration and tiredness had bubbled its way up and out, and allowed me to go on. I didn't know this at the time, as I hadn't yet been diagnosed, but this was a classic autistic meltdown. It felt awful at the time, but it released all the anxiety and allowed me to go on.

I spotted a construction truck a few meters away and slowly made my way toward it, where I asked directions to Bramber. Apparently, they had just finished building a new trail alongside the riverbank, which explained why my guidebook's map didn't coincide with the reality I was seeing. The builders explained which path I needed to follow to get to both Upper Beeding and Bramber, the two villages on either side of the River Adur. The walk was supposedly fifteen minutes, but I lost count of time as I walked. I hobbled tiredly down the trail until I reached the main road, grateful that I was close to my destination.

An older man with a small girl who appeared to be his granddaughter smiled at me as I walked up the stairs to the road. The man recommended that I stop off at a nearby candy shop for ice cream. I smiled and nodded, and then blatantly ignored his advice. All I wanted was my hotel. And I was almost there.

I turned left and headed slowly down the road toward my hotel, which once again was on the far end of the tiny village. I could see the ruins of Bramber Castle off in the distance, and I passed by the pretty little St. Mary's House, which was considered the best example of a 15th Century timber-framed house in Sussex. It looked gorgeous from the gateway, and I longed to enter, but instead, I plodded on to my hotel—no tourist attractions for me. The end was in sight!

The Evening

I was shown quickly to my room (first up two flights of stairs and then down another, along a hallway that seemed to go on forever), where I happily sat my backpack down on the floor and prepared to take a shower. I had my second meltdown of the day when I couldn't figure out how to operate the shower: yes, I broke down and cried once again. I eventually realized that to start the shower, I had to tug on a string hanging from the bathroom ceiling, which looked more like a light switch than a shower switch. Luckily, the water was as refreshing as always, and it improved my mood a bit.

Still, I was feeling so awful that I was seriously considering quitting the walk. I knew I had a long twenty-mile day for Day 6, and I just couldn't bear the thought of it. Day 5 was supposed to be Regeneration, but I felt terrible. The only upside was that I had swapped shoes for the day, and in doing so, had gained a whole new set of blisters while I gave the old ones a chance to rest and recover.

I was reminded that the card I had pulled for the following day was Inner Truth. Would quitting the Way be my Inner Truth? Was I not cut out for a 100-mile walk? Was this South Downs Way adventure going to turn out to be a failure? I had no idea.

I hobbled painfully downstairs for dinner on the outside patio, where I drank two more bottles of water as I waited for my meal. I debated about dessert, which I was tempted to eat because I was feeling terrible, but I decided not to. After limping back up and down the stairs to my room, I ended up going to bed very, very early. I checked my blisters one last time, slathered arnica cream all over my legs, and hoped I would fall asleep quickly so this day could finally come to a close. I just wanted it to be over.

As I lay in bed, I was still unsure as to whether I would continue on my journey or whether I would call it quits. At the same time, I was disappointed in myself for even thinking about quitting. I had been talking up this walk for the past couple of months. Walking was my thing. I loved it! How could I quit? Impossible! I wasn't a quitter. I was an avid walker. Wasn't I?

I knew the importance of mindset, and I was very much aware that entertaining thoughts of quitting was dangerous. Years ago, when I had first started running, I signed up for a marathon. It was slow going, and I was the last in the race, slowly plodding along. The spectators' cheers kept me going, but I felt pressured by the van that drove slowly behind me, marking me as the last of the runners. My thoughts had gotten more and more dismal as I passed each mile marker. Rather than feeling proud of myself for participating in a marathon just six months after starting to run, I was embarrassed to be last. I had prepared for this. I had trained for the event. Why did I have to be last? In the end, I gave up, just a couple of kilometers before the end of the race. I was tired and worn out, and it took years for me to understand that it was merely my poor mindset that had led me to quit.

I didn't want to repeat my mistake now, yet I couldn't imagine putting myself through the hell of walking twenty miles the following day. Walking no longer felt like the lovely spiritual and meditative exercise that it usually did. It was a torture that I was willingly subjecting myself to, and I felt torn between continuing ahead and quitting where I was. The prospect of quitting brought forth a whole new dilemma, though: there was no train station in either of the villages. Returning home from this point would inevitably involve a long and complicated route. Was there even a bus stop in any of these villages? I had no idea.

It wasn't until three weeks after I returned from my South Downs Way walk that I learned that this had been the hottest July day since records began: a sweltering 36.7° C (98° F). It was no wonder that I had suffered so much on Day 5 of my walk, trudging along that stage of the Way...and it was no surprise that this was the only day where I almost gave up on my walk. This day was an excellent lesson to check the weather reports daily, to better prepare for each day's walk. I might have had a little more compassion for myself if I had known just how hot it was. As it was, I went to sleep still undecided as to what I would do the next morning.

DAY 6

Bluebell–Inner Truth was the day's theme. The previous evening, I had gone to bed wondering if quitting the South Downs Way would be my Inner Truth. I seriously questioned whether was I cut out for a 100-mile walk. It hadn't seemed that much when I planned the trip, but it was turning out to be much more challenging than I had expected. Was my Inner Truth the fact that I was a quitter? Or would it be something even worse? Or—hopefully—would it be something better?

The Morning

It was clear that the Regeneration had happened overnight. My aching muscles felt like new, and the work I had done on my blisters seemed to have paid off. I headed downstairs for an early breakfast at 7 am, because I wanted to get a very early start to my day. I abandoned all thoughts of quitting once I saw how good I felt. I resolved to put my pack together and get ready for an early start on the road. I had a long walk ahead of me, and I wanted to get going as soon as possible. I was excited about my new outlook on the South Downs Way and anxious to get back on the trail and out in nature. I was most definitely *not* a quitter.

An early start, however, was not possible. Breakfast took forever. No one was downstairs when I went to the breakfast room, and then it took ages for them to bring me my food once I ordered it. I didn't dare ask for a sandwich to take with me; it appeared more sensible to head down to the village shop in Upper Beeding and get something there. I also wanted to get some extra Compeed just in case my blisters flared up again... or worse, I developed new ones. I wasn't interested in taking chances. This was, after all, the big twenty-mile day.

After breakfast, I dressed up my blisters in Compeed and got ready to go. It took ages to check out of the hotel because they had marked everything as paid, though I knew that my dinner hadn't been. Another employee was called, and he eventually sorted everything out for me. I rushed out the door as soon as I settled my bill, eager to make up for the lost time.

From there, I headed straight to Upper Beeding to find something for lunch. There was a relatively large (by South Downs Way standards) store where I found a sandwich, but no Compeed. The shop manager didn't even know what I was talking about, which I found strange for a village store located just off the South Downs. Surely they had walkers come through here regularly? This detour to pick up lunch took another 20 minutes, after which I was able to finally head down on the riverside trail to get back to the South Downs Way. This time, I headed confidently down the path, knowing exactly where I was going.

The Walk

The 20 miles from Bramber to Lewes passes up Truleigh Hill, home to a youth hostel, before continuing over Edburton Hill,

Fulking Hill, and on to the Devil's Dyke, a dry valley, before heading on to Newtimber Hill, a National Trust property. Then it's on to Pyecombe, past the Jack & Jill windmills of Clayton, and over the open hills toward Ditchling Beacon, home to a National Trust car park which boasts an ice cream van with refreshments. From there, it's a short walk to the turnoff to Lewes, which is three miles off the Way.

I felt completely recovered from the night before, but I was still nervous about the long 20-mile day I had ahead of me. I had calculated and re-calculated, and at the snail's pace I had been walking, it looked like it would take me twelve hours to reach Lewes, my next destination. This terrified me. Considering that I hadn't started walking until past 8:30 am, that meant I wouldn't get in until that same time in the evening. That was cutting it way too close to sundown for my taste, even though there was still light in the sky until almost ten each evening.

I considered taking a shortcut to Lewes, which was three miles off the Way. I had done bits of this path a few years prior, and I recognized a pub on the outskirts of Plumpton, just off the Way. I could take a detour down there and then take a bus or a taxi to Lewes. There was even a rail station in Plumpton, and I could take a train from there to Lewes. I reasoned that because the town was three miles off the Way, that wouldn't be cheating. With this shortcut in mind, I felt a little relieved about the day ahead. I was satisfied that I had plenty of options to make things easier.

There were signs everywhere stating that some trail in the area was closed, but it wasn't clear to me whether it was the path I was on or some other. I continued down the new riverside trail until I reached an orange blockade that marked the closure of the route I was on. I maneuvered my way around it and continued toward the sign that marked the South Downs Way, to the left and to the right. I wasn't taking any chances of missing the correct trail, and I wasn't interested in making a detour that might get me lost.

This point is where I realized how I had strayed from the Way at the end of the previous day, when I had my mini-break-down, fearing I had gotten lost. Because I was joining the South Downs Way from another point of access, it took some time to get reoriented. I stopped to evaluate for a moment, which was the right direction, and then I was confidently off. It was 9 am, much later than I had initially intended to start. If it did take me twelve hours to get to Lewes, I would barely make it in before dark. But I was Regenerated! I felt like a new person this morning, and everything was looking up.

The weather was beautifully overcast, and there was a refreshing cool breeze. It was a gorgeous, gray, misty morning. That alone made me optimistic about my prospects of actually arriving at Lewes that afternoon, even if I did get in late. Because I was feeling so much better that morning, I resolved to push myself to walk at my usual speedy walking pace, or at least as close to it as I could manage. My daily mantra started early on this day. I turned it into a four-syllable phrase I could click along to with my poles: "In-ner Tru-uth, In-ner Tru-uth."

I crossed a busy road, then headed up a grassy hill. As always, the trail started by heading steadily uphill, toward the Truleigh Hill Youth Hostel. The Beeding Hill National Trust property was off to my right, and there were exceptional views of the Adur Valley all around. The sky continued to get darker, which gave me hope that the day's forecast for rain would prove right. When I reached the hostel, I filled one of my water bottles at the tap outside. I was carrying one less bottle than I had the day before: there were two taps along this stage of the Way, and there would be one ice cream van that would most likely have water. I was gambling on the weather and the water taps to keep my weight down in my pack today. Hopefully, less weight would help me get through the 20 miles.

I was sailing along at what felt like a speedy pace—it was remarkable the difference that the weather made. I had decided to walk as quickly as I could and to take fewer breaks so that I would arrive at Lewes sometime before 9 pm. I wondered about the man whom I kept crossing paths with on the trail, the one who would usually speed-walk past me. I also hadn't seen Maggie and Martin the previous night at dinner; they were staying in Upper Beeding rather than Bramber. I wondered where they were on the trail, as they were also concerned about the long day. Would they have started earlier than I did? For the first time, I felt a bit lonely, out of contact with the only other people I knew who were on the Way. I also felt more vulnerable than usual on this long day, even though the weather had improved.

The trail I was on consisted of a narrow dirt track that cut through an open hill that was blanketed in short green grass. There was the occasional small shrub here and there, but it was mostly open territory. The mist and fog were now so thick I couldn't see more than a few meters in front of me. Everything beyond that was covered with a dense blanket of gorgeous fog. It was like walking in a cloud, and I had never been so grateful for such gray weather. I happily continued onward along Fulking Hill.

It started to rain, and for once on a walk, I welcomed the wet weather. I continued until it was clear that I was going to get drenched. The right side of my body was soaked through, as the wind was blowing from that direction. I pulled out my waterproof pants and jacket and covered my backpack with its waterproof cover. As I was hastily pulling on my waterproofs, the man I had been crossing paths with passed me. A few minutes down the trail, he stopped to pull out his backpack cover, and I passed him.

I was very aware of his walking speed, and I wondered whether I could keep up with him. I was confident that if I could match his pace, I could get into Lewes at a decent time. I clicked along with my poles, repeating my daily mantra to keep the rhythm and to make sure my pace was regular. From there, I came down a little hill, where I crossed a road and went into Saddlescombe Farm, where there was another water tap. This time, I didn't bother to fill up. There was also a walker's cafe with food, but I didn't stop there, either. I was on a mission to reach Lewes at a decent hour. No rest for me.

I was determined to keep on without stopping, but it had ceased raining, and I knew I had to remove my waterproofs, or else I'd risk getting too hot. At this point, the group of runners passed me. By this time, I had learned that they were Gurkhas, a group of Nepalese army men who formed part of a division of the British army and that every year they ran a race from the Queen Elizabeth Country Park (which I had passed on my second day of walking) to Brighton. This would probably be the last day they passed me on the trail, as they would need to turn off the South Downs Way very soon to get down to the coast.

There was another climb to the top of Newtimber Hill, and I followed the unnamed walking man, trying to keep the same distance from him and not fall too far behind. Keeping my pace was necessary today, and it appeared that the lighter weight in my pack (due to less water and to a bag of figs I had deliberately left back at the hotel) and the cool, rainy weather were working in my favor. I was managing to keep up with the man, whom I had seen every day since Cocking but whose name I hadn't yet learned—nor had I asked for it.

Walking Man stopped along the trail, and I clicked past him, trying to keep a brisk pace now that I no longer had him as my marker. I crossed the busy A23 road via a bridge and headed up through Pyecombe, which was the village I had been trying to find a B&B in when I was considering extending my walk to nine days. I now realized just how close it was to

Bramber, and if I were to stop now, it would have made for a short walking day.

From there, the path headed steadily uphill through a golf course. Once I reached the top of the hill, I took my first real break, sitting down to check my guidebook at a point where the trail turned left so I could see how things were going. It seemed like I was making perfect time, which was a relief. I had a drink of water and then got back up.

The trail turned left, continued past some stables, then turned right again, climbing steeply uphill toward Ditchling Beacon. Walking Man caught up to me at one point. We walked together for a bit, discussing our high hopes for the ice cream van that awaited us at the top. He had the same Trailblazer guidebook as I, which promised an ice cream van in season with cold drinks in the National Trust car park, and we were both longing for a break and for something cool to drink or eat. I had never looked forward to ice cream this much in all my life.

The rain had stopped, and the sun had come out a bit, but it was still damp, and it was thankfully nowhere near as hot as on previous days. As we approached Ditchling Beacon, the awaited ice cream van was in its place in the parking lot, and we both ordered bottles of water and ice cream and then walked off to eat it on a small hill in the center of the parking lot.

We discussed how the walk had been going for each of us, and Walking Man confessed that he wasn't sure whether or not long-distance walking was for him. I agreed, and this was the first time I had said it out loud: I was no longer sure whether I wanted to do a walk like this ever again. Somehow, admitting it out loud finally made it real. I was simultaneously relieved and disappointed that my dream of annual long-distance walking holidays appeared to be over.

I had started the first three days on the South Downs with the certainty that I wanted to do all the long walks on my list and more. Now, I felt pretty sure I'd be canceling the Camino de Santiago walk I had blocked out in my calendar for the following year as soon as I returned home. It no longer felt appealing. I knew that plenty of other people walked the Camino with less preparation than I had, but I also knew that a more extended walk would be even more difficult than what I was experiencing now. What was the tipping point at which long-distance walks went from pleasure to pain? I had no idea, and I didn't relish the thought of experimenting to find out.

I decided that this revelation was my Inner Truth for the day: I was done as a long-distance walker. Somehow, this was a relief.

From there, we continued walking together, talking a bit as we went. We were still on the top of a ridge with open views to both sides of the trail. I was pleased to be able to keep up with his pace, though just barely. It was a bit of a stretch for me, and I wondered if I would have to pay for my fast walking in the late afternoon. I was afraid to crash and burn after pushing myself so hard early in the day. Ditchling Beacon appeared to be the halfway point for our walk, and I had reached it much earlier in the day than I expected, which confused me. It was also puzzling that after Ditchling Beacon, there was just one map page in my book before the turnoff to Lewes.

It all seemed like things were going far too well, which was surely too good to be true. I was way ahead of schedule, which made me wonder if perhaps I was reading the map wrong or if I had grossly miscalculated in some way. The track headed along the ridge of the Downs, with excellent views once more to both sides. Walking Man stopped for some reason, and I went on. I was baffled, and I needed to figure this out on my own.

I passed between the green fields of sheep. There was the odd shrub dotted here and there throughout the landscape, but it was mostly wide-open land. The day was still cool and pleasant.

I was still determined to take the turnoff to The Half Moon pub at Plumpton and get a taxi or a bus to Lewes, but as I happily clicked on at my speedy pace, I reached a sign that indicated 3 miles to Lewes. That didn't seem right, so I sat down for a break and brought out my trusty guidebook. I studied the map and confirmed that I was clearly at the point for the Lewes turn off, and had missed the detour to Plumpton altogether. It had been a steep track to my left that headed downhill off the ridge toward the little village. So it seemed that there would be no train from Plumpton to Lewes; I would be walking there directly.

I had some water and pulled out my sandwich, as I was starting to get a bit hungry. This pause gave Walking Man time to catch up to me, and he confirmed that we were, indeed, just three miles from Lewes. He was heading another way, turning off the trail at the A27 road, which was also three miles on, though down a different path. I debated whether to walk the three miles to Lewes or to walk to the A27 and get a bus or taxi. Then, I could get transport back from Lewes the next day and end up back on the Way.

I decided to head straight off the South Downs Way and walk to Lewes on foot, a decision that I would later regret. It was an easy trail, flat at first, and then heading downhill along a public bridleway. There were few people out today, which appeared to be usual for a weekday on the South Downs. The path was wide and comfortable until it gradually got narrower and narrower until it was so tiny I could no longer use my poles for walking. But it didn't matter. I was less than three miles from Lewes, which was a clear enough goal to complete.

The trail seemed to go on forever. It was a long three miles, partly because I had finally allowed myself to slow my pace and take it easy for this last bit. It was clear that I was going to get in around 4 pm, and that was about five hours earlier than I had initially estimated. I was elated yet still confused and decided to give myself all the extra time I needed, though my feet were starting to ache.

I eventually reached the edge of Lewes, coming down a hill alongside the Lewes Prison, where I brought out my guidebook to check the map. I headed downhill toward the High Street, which I followed straight through the town. Lewes High Street is a busy road lined with shops, and I hadn't seen this many people since I had started my journey in Winchester. I saw a pharmacy and headed in to get some extra Compeed since I hadn't been able to find any that morning in Bramber. Compeed in the pack, I resumed my course to the B&B, which I quickly discovered, after having traversed the entire town of Lewes. I was simultaneously elated at having arrived by 4 pm, but still very, very confused. Had I walked twenty miles? My pedometer confirmed that I had, and even a bit more, including my walk through town. But how had I done it so quickly?

The Evening

I had plenty of time to rest and relax in my B&B before walking a short distance to the end of the street, where my host had recommended a pub for dinner. I showered and lounged on my bed, pondering over maps and my guidebook, unable to decide what to do the following morning to get back on the South Downs Way. I was frustrated that I had walked a total of four miles off the Way and annoyed that there was no easy path to return without adding four miles onto the following day's walk.

I walked a half-block down the street to the pub and debated between sitting outside in the garden or inside in the shade. It didn't take long for me to opt for the cool depths of the pub, where I sat and watched a stream of people head in for dinner until the small pub was almost full. I chose the sword-fish with vegetables, which was light and delicious, and I followed it with a berry crumble with custard, which was so huge I couldn't finish it.

As the pub wasn't yet full, I lingered at my table, typing up the day's walk on my iPad. I kept an eye on the empty tables to make sure I wasn't taking up space that the pub needed for paying diners. Eventually, I finished my day's writing and was ready to walk back to my B&B and settle in for the evening. Aching, I stood from my table and slowly hobbled the half block back to my accommodation and up the stairs to my room, where I resumed studying my options for the following day.

I was still astounded that I had walked twenty miles in what felt like record time. How could it be that I had estimated arriving as late as 9 pm, and ended up knocking on the door of my B&B as early as 4 pm? Something magical had happened to help me along my way. I knew that the weather had been in my favor, and that had made all the difference in the world.

It was all going so well that I couldn't believe I had considered quitting my walk the night before. What I had expected to be a hellish twenty-mile walk had ended up being surprisingly manageable. I was so happy that I had believed in myself enough to give it a go. It had been much, much more comfortable than the previous day, which made me look forward to the following day's walk.

DAY 7

LEWES TO ALFRISTON: 13 MILES (21 KM)

B lack Bryony–Vitality was the oracle for the day. Two days ago, on Regeneration day, I hadn't felt refreshed in the morning. Regeneration had only happened during that night as I recovered from the day's walk. This day's theme was Vitality, and I certainly wasn't feeling that. Would I have to wait until the next morning to feel a sense of vitality?

The Morning

After calculating and recalculating the best way to get back on the Way and not still being satisfied with any of the options, I went to bed a bit later than I intended. Still, I woke up feeling rested and refreshed, or so I thought. The moment I stretched my legs and toes and set foot on the ground, I realized that for the first time, my aches hadn't gone away by the morning.

I knew that the previous day had been the longest day of the week, but this was puzzling. I had expected to feel better by the morning. This lack of recovery after the previous day's walk meant that I needed to once again reevaluate my options for returning to the Way. If I wanted to return the same route I had come into Lewes, I'd end up with a seventeen-mile walk today, and that wouldn't be easy if the weather forecast for a sunny day were accurate.

I spent all morning obsessing about how to get back to the Way to take up my path again. It occupied my thoughts while getting ready and then while having breakfast. I brought a map downstairs and asked my B&B host what she recommended. She pointed out two trails that would take me even further down the Way, making me miss out on several miles of the official trail. Neither of those was an option, as I didn't want to miss anything. It would feel like cheating. I wanted to experience the complete official version of the South Downs Way, and I seemed to have forgotten the fact that I had taken that detour up Beacon Hill on the second day rather than going all the way around the hill.

As I saw it, I had four options I was willing to consider. I could retrace my steps back up to the main trail precisely as I had before, adding four miles onto a thirteen-mile walk. I could get a taxi up to the stables, which were located halfway up the bridleway leading to the South Downs Way, adding just two miles onto the thirteen-mile walk. I could get a taxi to the Half Moon pub in Plumpton and then head steeply uphill back to the Way and retrace some of my steps from the previous day before arriving once more at the place where I detoured down to Lewes. Finally, I could take a bus to Housedean Farm, which was located directly on the Way at the base of a big hill.

Every option that didn't lead to the precise point where I left off the Way the previous day felt like cheating, and I didn't much like any of the options. I wished I had followed the other 3-mile path down to Housedean Farm and the A27 the day before, instead of taking the route I took to Lewes. I could have picked up a taxi or a bus on the A27 and gotten into Lewes that way. And then I'd have a perfect point to return to along the Way. It would have been seamless.

Because this was the first morning I hadn't fully recovered from the previous day's walk, I was worried about adding extra miles to my thirteen-mile walk to Alfriston. Everything ached, and the ibuprofen I had taken in the morning wasn't doing much to help. I knew my body wasn't up for another twenty-mile day, or anything close to it. When I packed everything up and got ready to go, I was leaning toward the bus option, but still wasn't convinced.

After coming down the stairs to head out, I saw Maggie and Martin having breakfast in the dining room. I was happy to see them and asked what they were planning to do, but their plan didn't help me at all. They had come off the Way at Kingston-near-Lewes to take a taxi to Lewes. They were planning to take a taxi back and pick up the trail at the same point this morning. It seemed that everyone had planned their access to Lewes better than I had.

In the end, I decided it was best for my wellbeing and for my feet to take the bus to Housedean Farm on the A27, but I also felt like a big cheater. The bit of the Way I'd be missing would be a three-mile walk down the same hill I had descended the previous afternoon on another path. So it wasn't *too much* of a cheat. I had walked those three miles on the same hill; it just wasn't on the official path. But it was still nagging at me.

The Walk

The thirteen miles from Lewes to Alfriston wind up and down through grassy fields, passing close to Kingston-near-Lewes before heading over Swanborough Hill, Iford Hill, and down through the village of Southease, home to a church and water tap, a new youth hostel, and a rail station. This part of the Way slopes up and down through farmland before it passes over

Bostal Hill and heads down to the pretty village of Alfriston.
This is a day of expansive views in all directions.

After a stop at Boots to pick up more ibuprofen, I headed
straight for the bus station and got on a bus that was departing
for Brighton, stopping at Housedean Farm along the way. My
mind gremlins were chanting "cheater, cheater," and I feared
they would continue the entire day. I was frustrated with
myself, even though I knew I was making the best decision.

This situation really pointed the finger at my lack of flexibility. I hate straying from my original plan, and that's precisely
what had happened here. Things weren't working out as I had
planned, and I didn't like it one bit. I wished I had opted to stay
somewhere closer to the South Downs Way, rather than coming
all the way off the path into Lewes for the night. What had I
been thinking? And why hadn't I taken the other three-mile
trail down to the A27? I was mentally beating myself up over my
wrong decision, yet there was nothing I could do to rectify it.

It was another hot, sunny day on the Downs, but there was
a slightly more refreshing breeze than on previous days. This
was possibly due to the fact that I was now a lot closer to the
sea. I could see it clearly, off to the right, no longer just a vague
gray-blue haze in the distance. This day, like all days on the
South Downs, was full of sloping trails up and down the hills.

I now had lots of energy, but my feet were still aching a bit,
which was a constant distraction. I was torn between wanting
to walk fast so I could arrive earlier and spend less time on my
feet and slowing down to enjoy my next to the last day on the
Downs. My special time in this magical world was soon coming
to an end. Part of me was looking forward to returning home
free of pain, and part of me did not want it to be over.

I was still confused about whether I was actually a long-
distance walker or just a daywalker at heart. The idea of going
out for a 5-6 hour day walk was so appealing: waking up early

in my own bed, heading out to a trail, and coming home in the evening, knowing I could rest the following day. The problem with long-distance trails was that they involved relentless days of long walks, one after the other—and with lots of weight on my back.

The trail wound around and around the hills, with a view of Lewes always off in the distance. My mind gremlins continued to taunt me: "cheater, cheater." Eventually, a couple of hours into the walk, my feet were aching so much, and I was so hot and sweaty that I no longer felt like a cheater. I would be walking my thirteen miles today, and it wouldn't be easy. Surely I couldn't be a cheater if I were suffering that much. I stopped mentally beating myself up.

Eventually, the path came down into the village of Southease, consisted of just a church and a handful of houses. I headed straight to the Church of St. Peter, a Saxon church dating back to the 11th Century with a round Norman tower from the 12th Century. The church sits on a triangular village green surrounded by cottages on the other two sides. There were benches outside the churchyard where I could rest and a water tap where I could fill my bottles. I sat down in the shade to rest my feet, and I decided to have my lunch.

A couple was sitting on the bench next to me. They were doing day walks on the Way, based out of Alfriston, and lived nearby in Hampshire. They were approaching the South Downs in bits and pieces, which of course, made things more manageable—and less painful. It was thanks to them that I learned that it was the Gurkhas I had crossed paths with as they did their annual run along the Downs.

I didn't take the time to explore the church, or even to see if it was open, which was odd because I always enjoyed the musty coolness of old churches. St. Peter's houses the remains of wall paintings that date back to the 13th Century, which used to cover the entire church. They were covered up at some point, then uncovered once again in the 1930s.

After lunch, I took two more ibuprofen in the hopes that they would alleviate the foot pain, and then I stood to head back on the trail. I crossed the River Ouse (the same river where Virginia Woolf drowned herself) and discovered a brand new youth hostel with a courtyard cafe. I had just eaten my lunch, but I entered to see if they had cold drinks and possibly ice cream. I settled down in the quiet courtyard with a fizzy elderflower drink and an ice cream. This time, I was all alone, so I took my boots and socks and let my feet air out.

What a difference it makes to take off hiking boots during a break! My feet felt fresh and cool, and my socks had a chance to dry out. I lingered in the shade of my courtyard table with my elderflower drink. When I got up to continue on the Way, my feet felt better, as though they were ready to tackle the second half of my journey. Several signs indicated that Southease was the halfway point for the day, with just six and a half miles to go to Alfriston.

From there, I crossed over the tracks at the Southease rail station, which was a surprising location for trains to stop since I was in the middle of nowhere. It was a miracle that this station hadn't been closed in the Beeching Cuts. I then crossed a bridge over the main road to head back into the Downs. The village of Southease, with its church and youth hostel, was the only major landmark on the trail this day. I eventually passed the telecom towers on Beddingham Hill, which I had seen earlier in the morning when a man walking his dog indicated to me that my journey would pass by them.

My feet were tired. I stopped alongside the trail to sit and rest near Firle Beacon, which as a Marilyn, was the highest peak in today's walk. In Britain and Ireland, a Marilyn is defined as a peak with a prominence above 150 meters (492.1 ft). This rather unusual name for a type of hill was coined by Alan

Dawson in his 1992 book *The Relative Hills of Britain*. The classification was meant to be in contrast to the Munro classification of Scottish mountains that rise above 3,000 feet (914.4 m). The word Munro is pronounced the same as Monroe, which, of course, is the last name of a famous Marilyn.

Firle Beacon was clearly the site of early settlements, as there are several Bronze Age round barrows in the area, and also a Neolithic long barrow. There is a bowl barrow on the Beacon itself, within which two cremation urns were discovered when it was excavated in 1820. Today, Firle Beacon is a popular site for hang gliding and paragliding.

Here, I crossed paths with an older couple who were walking the eastern half of the Way and had hired a transport service for their packs. They looked quite refreshed and chipper. Somehow that felt like cheating at my age, though I conceded that transport for my backpack would have made the whole journey a lot easier. However, there was something profoundly satisfying about the simplicity of traveling with all of my things in a backpack. I enjoyed arriving at each day's accommodation to unpack my things, use what I needed, then repack them the following morning.

I continued up and then down a hill, where I rested once again, sitting on a large concrete block and pulling up my feet alongside me. I thought my feet would feel better if they were elevated, though, in reality, it didn't make much of a difference. I was no longer on Firle Beacon, but the surrounding area was still popular with gliders. I watched a group of paragliders who were busy setting up and taking off from a nearby field. The grazing sheep bleated anxiously, clearly displeased at the disturbance.

I climbed up Bostal Hill, where the trail was dotted with tumuli on both sides of the path. From there, I headed down a sloping trail toward Alfriston, lined with brambles and bushes. I was close to the village, but I couldn't actually see it. Once I reached the pretty little village of Alfriston, I headed straight to my B&B, which was located on the outskirts of the village, about a ten-minute walk from the edge of the village.

My feet were killing me, and I stopped along the way to check my map to make sure I was headed in the right direction. I was so close to my B&B, and I couldn't bear the thought of walking the wrong way and then having to backtrack. I eventually saw the sign for Riverdale House, and I hiked slowly up the steep driveway, eager to settle in. It was my last night on the trail.

The Evening

My room was nice enough at Riverdale House, but I had been expecting much more for the price. This was the most expensive accommodation I had reserved for my journey, as all of the less expensive accommodation had been booked by the time I organized my trip. There were three twin beds in the room, and I had a separate bathroom that I imagine I would have shared with other people if there had been anyone else on my floor. In other B&Bs, I had had an en suite bathroom for less than half of what I was paying here.

Still, I was used to a shared bathroom, and it was good enough for my needs. I was hungry, and I made a quick cup of tea and ate the two biscuits in the room. After showering, I rested in my room. Then I called down to The George Inn to make a reservation for that evening's dinner. I lounged around some more, then prepared myself mentally to limp the ten minutes back into the village to eat. My feet were in terrible shape.

Returning to the village ended up being easier than I had imagined. My shower and rest had served as a kind of reset button for my energy levels, and I was able to easily manage the journey to my dinner destination. Once again, I felt the need for something filling and substantial, and I chose the lamb burger and fries. The pub was dark, and I felt like being outside, so I decided on a table in the back garden.

The moment I sat down, I realized I had been there before. It didn't take long before I remembered the exact table where I had sat, and when: it was a long day walk from Glynde to Seaford for Agustín's birthday back in 2011 or 2012. I was shocked, as I hadn't recognized Alfriston village that afternoon as I walked through it. I had been so intent on finding my B&B and getting off my feet that I hadn't recognized it at all.

I had a leisurely dinner, enjoying my lamb burger as the pub garden slowly filled with people. As usual, I kept my eye on how many empty tables remained while I typed away on my iPad. When I saw that I could stretch out my stay no longer, I slowly eased myself up from the table and headed out of the pub.

I explored the village a bit before limping back to the B&B. Alfriston is one of those gorgeous little English villages, made up of a collection of Tudor wood-beamed cottages lined up along the High Street. My guidebook proclaimed that it was a candidate for "prettiest village on the South Downs Way," and this was true: it looked like something out of a fairy tale. It was well worth spending some time exploring, and I resolved to have another look around the following morning when my feet had recovered.

DAY 8

Horsetail–Sweep Away the Old was my daily oracle. I wondered what that would mean. I loved the idea of letting go of things that I no longer needed—of decluttering my thoughts and feelings. Perhaps it would be a day for me to declutter my mind? I couldn't imagine what else it might be.

The Morning

My room was up at the top of the house and had two windows, which made the room light and airy. Luckily, the weather cooled down at night, and I was able to sleep well with such good ventilation in the room.

I was feeling very ambivalent about nearing the end of my journey. Walking was once again meditation-like for me: there were moments when I verbally recorded my thoughts to make sure I remembered to write them down in the evenings, but most of the time, I wasn't really thinking about anything. It was pure relaxation—and pain—all at the same time.

I was looking forward to getting home and seeing Agustín

and our kittens, whom I missed. I was also looking forward to pain-free days. And at the same time, I was sorry that this was all coming to a close. On this final morning on the South Downs, I was experiencing a bizarre combination of relief and sadness.

The past seven days had brought me deeper and deeper into this magical world of the South Downs, and deeper into my own inner world. Deeper into what felt like an alternate reality that was leading me toward the final day: Sweep Away the Old.

The Walk

The thirteen miles from Alfriston to Eastbourne along the coastal route start out by cutting first through farmland, heading through the Cuckmere Valley before traversing the woodland of Friston Forest, and then passing through Exceat, the starting point of the Seven Sisters Country Park. This marks the final stage of the South Downs Way, home to some very, very different scenery: open, rolling hills with vertical white chalk cliffs down to the water below. This part of the journey looks nothing like the previous days.

I departed my B&B at precisely 9 am after a leisurely breakfast, which was served in the conservatory. I headed back into the village to get a sandwich at the deli, which everyone recommended. They had a great variety of sandwiches that could be ordered, but I was told I'd have to wait ten minutes, as the deli woman wasn't quite ready. She was busy organizing everything.

After standing around for a couple of minutes, I headed outside to wait. I was anxious to get on the trail, and eventually, I decided that a sandwich wasn't worth waiting for. I could see from the map that there were several different places where I could get lunch along the route. This appeared to be the stage with the most cafes, water taps, and public bathrooms, which was a relief after so many days of searching for a decent bush to hide behind. It did make sense, though, as this was the final stage of the Way, and we were approaching Eastbourne.

Just at the edge of the village, the South Downs Way splits into two: the inland route via Jevington and the coastal route via Seven Sisters, which is the one I chose. The path followed the River Cuckmere through a grassy field dotted with wildflowers. The morning had started out overcast, but the sun was now out, and it promised to be yet another warm day.

Cows were everywhere, it seemed. Many of them blocked the path and were in no hurry to move out of my way. I started to weave in and out among them. There were calves nursing, and there were several mid-sized cows that weren't calves yet weren't fully grown either. Perhaps they had been born the previous year? I had no idea how long it took cows to reach their full size, but later research showed that it took two years. I was worried about disturbing the mothers with their calves, but they didn't seem bothered by my presence, so I continued through the field as quickly and as quietly as possible.

The trail left the riverbank and turned down a narrow alleyway that led to the village of Litlington, which was signposted as being one mile from Alfriston. One mile down, nine miles to go. Litlington is a tiny village that is home to the Plough & Harrow pub and the Litlington Tea Gardens & Nursery. It was too early in the day for me to be interested in either of the two. If you turn left as you come onto the main road of Litlington and head past the tea gardens, you can visit the church of St Michael the Archangel, which is near the Long Man Brewery. The main part of the church dates back to about 1150 AD. Unfortunately, this wasn't on the map in my guidebook, so I didn't find this out until later.

It looked like I had an easy day ahead of me. The trail was well marked, and there had been benches everywhere that morning. From Litlington, the path began a steep ascent through a field before continuing across another field. Here, the sign wasn't clear, and I stopped to ask two other walkers which way they thought it might be. They pulled out a map, and together we reconfirmed the correct direction.

Once out of the field, the trail led up a long flight of stairs into Friston Forest, which was cool, shady, and breezy—a welcome change after so many days of scorching sunshine in the open fields. The trail wound down through the tiny settlement of Westdean, where once again, it was not well marked, and I had to confirm the correct route with both the previous couple and another couple I had seen in the last two days.

Westdean—also spelled West Dean—is a tiny hamlet of pretty little cottages set around a small duck pond. The Grade I listed church of All Saints is mostly Norman, with the oldest parts of the building dating back to Saxon times. Westdean All Saints is one of the five Cuckmere Valley churches, which also include St Andrew's of Alfriston, The Good Shepherd of Lullington, St Michael the Archangel of Litlington, and St Peter ad Vincula of Folkington.

The path took us up a steep flight of steps through the trees, and I realized for the second time that morning how awkward it was to go up woodland stairs. I had no reason to complain, though: I was grateful for the lush shade that the trees provided. The woodland was short lived, though, as the trail soon came out into the open.

At the top, I had a view through the bushes of Exceat and the Seven Sisters Country Park. I waited for a large group of people to step over the low fence ahead of me so they could continue down the trail, and then I headed over it myself. There was another large group of Italian tourists with a guide who was explaining to them about the Cuckmere Valley below. This estuary is apparently one of the only river mouths in Southeast England that have not been disturbed by development. The river snaked back and forth through a green grassy valley, flanked on both sides by low hills.

Exceat is home to an information center, public toilets, and a water fountain to refill bottles. I took advantage of the toilets, but not the water tap, as I had enough water, and I didn't want to weigh myself down on my last day since there were so many places to stop. Upon heading toward the facilities, I noticed a sign that read three miles to Alfriston, ten to Eastbourne, which surprised me: the total walk for today was supposed to be only eleven miles. Apparently, the last day's hike would be longer than I had expected. Either that or the sign was wrong, which I doubted. Oh well, at least it would make the last day a bit longer. I was in no rush to arrive.

There were people everywhere, which was a shocking contrast to my previous days along the South Downs. The Seven Sisters Country Park was clearly a tourist attraction, and there were people from all parts of the world. Some were browsing through the information center, others were walking through the valley. I hadn't seen so many people since I started the Way, and it was a shock to my system.

This day's walk was clearly going to be my transition back into normal society after so much solitude and quiet. I wondered if this day's theme, Sweep Away the Old, was about letting go of the magic I had experienced on the Way and transitioning back into everyday life. Or was it about letting go of even bigger things?

From there, the trail wound up, down, and around to the start of the Seven Sisters, which are a series of undulating white chalk cliffs by the sea. The guidebook promised a roller coaster ride up and down the cliffs, which my B&B host that morning had assured me would be an easy walk. I was up for something easy after seven days of walking.

Unfortunately, I lost count of the sisters as the trail sloped up and down, up and down. The sea breeze was a bit gusty in moments, leading me to loop the elastic wristbands of my poles around my wrists for the first time ever in fear of losing them. The trail was open grassland, with wildflowers and small shrubs dotted here and there. The cliffs ended abruptly in a long drop down to the sea. At some points, you could walk right up to the edge; at others, there was a wire fence to keep people away from the eroding cliff.

I reached Sarsen Stone, a landmark on my map that was surrounded by a bench, and sat down to rest, putting my feet up. I consulted my guidebook and learned that I was already on the fifth sister. Just two to go, and then I would reach Birling Gap, the next landmark on the day's journey. I was in no rush to reach Eastbourne, as I was still sad to be ending my walk along the South Downs. I sat there peacefully, enjoying the breeze and watching the people passing by, then I got up to continue my journey.

The trail was so full of people that no one was greeting anyone anymore, as was the custom on the more rural parts of the South Downs. It felt so impersonal and busy and touristy. Most of the people were clearly day walkers, from what I could judge by their packs. I heard all sorts of languages coming from the people walking by: Japanese, Italian, Spanish. The Seven Sisters Country Park was a magnet for international tourists. It was summertime, the weather was gorgeous, and people had flocked to the coast.

The Way continued up and down, up and down, until I reached Birling Gap, where there was a cafe and bar run by the National Trust. It was full of people, but I decided to go in anyway and get something to eat and drink, as it appeared to be the obvious place for lunch. Plus, it would extend my day and delay my arrival in Eastbourne. I took everything outside on their seaside terrace to eat on a bench. The tables were packed, and one by one, the benches filled up, too. It seemed everyone had come out for the day, which wasn't a surprise, considering it was a Saturday. How things had changed from the days when I walked through the heart of the Downs.

I took my time eating, watching the other people as they walked by. Nearby was a horse tied to a post, his shirtless owner eating lunch at the table next to him. The horse attracted everyone who walked by: they all wanted to either pet him or to take a photo of him. He was clearly the attraction of the hour, and his tanned, tattooed, and leathery chested owner didn't seem to mind. This man was the most unique person I had seen so far on the way: from the waist up, he looked like he belonged on a motorcycle, not a horse, and from the waist down, he was decked out in proper riding gear. His presence was just another sign that I was approaching a more urban environment.

I finished my sandwich and put my feet up on the bench. I had been debating about whether to take off my boots or not but decided to keep them on. There were so many people around that it felt inappropriate to air my feet in what was essentially an outdoor cafe. I was no longer in the heart of the Downs; I was back in civilization. I lingered for a while before starting again on the trail.

Once my feet were feeling rested, I headed out of the National Trust cafe and back up the South Downs Way, climbing a sloping hill toward the Belle Tout Lighthouse B&B, which was right on the trail. It also had a snack bar with ice cream, which I walked straight past. I was saving my ice cream for the end of the Way, which was apparently marked with a kiosk.

The trail followed the grassy clifftops, heading up and down, over and over, until it began its final ascent toward Beachy Head, which was the highest point on the trail today, rising 535 feet (163 meters) above sea level. Sadly, this beautiful place has been a popular location for suicide attempts as far back as the 1600s. Currently, about 20 people each year commit suicide at Beachy Head. It's like the Golden Gate Bridge of Britain.

I found a lookout point with a circle of benches inside it, and I sat down, putting my feet up to rest. I knew that I had just a half-hour left on the Way, and I was trying to stretch things out as much as I could. I was so disappointed that my South Downs experience was coming to an end.

Eventually, I got up and walked on, following the path through scrubland with excellent views of the sea, and finally, a view of Eastbourne off in the distance. The track was now broad and open, and I really wasn't sure which way it was headed. There was no longer a clear trail. I saw a signpost off in the distance, and walked toward it. It was marked "Seaside SDW," so I followed that down to another signpost, which said nothing at all about the South Downs Way. I was no longer sure that I was on the right path, and I didn't want to stray from the official trail on the last remaining minutes of my journey.

I stopped to ask two women if I was actually on the official part of the South Downs Way. They pulled out a map to assure me that I was and asked me how long I had been walking. They were surprised that I had almost completed the entire 100 miles on my own and seemed impressed. I smiled and silently agreed with them that I was also surprised and impressed with myself, considering how close I had come to quitting just a couple of days prior.

I descended the final hill on a steep path, where I saw an information sign that declared the start (or the end, depending on how you look at it) of the South Downs Way. As I approached the bottom of the trail where it met the road, I saw a six-finger signpost that announced that it was 100 miles to Winchester. I had arrived. The women, who were heading in the same direction, offered to take a photograph of me by the sign. I readily agreed: anything to add some sort of celebration to the moment.

The end was anticlimactic, as I had feared. With tears welling in my eyes, I went into the kiosk at the base of the trail and ordered an ice cream and sat down to eat it. My feet were aching and tired. I had taken advantage of all the best rest spots and benches along the last stretch of the Way, but my feet were still tired. I had no doubt I would be calling a taxi to get to the rail station. I had completed the South Downs Way, and now I didn't want to walk one more step.

Sweep Away the Old had been the theme for this day, and I still had no idea what it was all about. What was I meant to sweep away? Or what had been swept away? What was this "Old" that I needed to get rid of? Was it old conceptions, ideas, beliefs? It was all still a mystery—the only daily theme that really didn't seem to make sense. Perhaps in walking the 100 miles from Winchester to Eastbourne, I had managed to let go of something old and unneeded. Only time would tell.

I ate the ice cream and sat there, reluctant to leave. I was hoping that some of the people I knew from the trail would finish their walk so I could say goodbye, though I knew that was wishful thinking. I had no idea where anyone else was on the path or whether they had finished before me.

I couldn't tear myself away from the South Downs Way. I had walked the full 100 miles, and now it was over. I certainly hadn't been expecting a diploma or a ceremony upon my arrival, but the ending seemed a bit abrupt. It was all very anti-climactic. Deep down, I had been hoping that I'd see all the people I had crossed paths with along the Way, and that we'd all congratulate each other on having finished. I hadn't said goodbye to any of them, and I felt strange about leaving the Way without seeing them again. But so it would be.

I leafed through my guidebook to pass the time, then disconnected airplane mode on my mobile phone, so I could send out all of the Instagram photos I had taken that day. I got up to get something to drink, so I could write up this chapter on my iPad, and eventually, the older couple I had crossed paths with the past two days arrived as well. We congratulated each other on finishing.

The sensation was weird: I had clearly returned to the Real World. The entire day had been a gradual acclimatization since the trail had been packed with weekend walkers from Exceat onward. But my adventure was finally over, and I had to accept it. I reluctantly dialed the number listed in my guidebook for Eastbourne Taxis, and patiently waited for one to arrive. It came all too soon.

The South Downs Way had been so much harder than I had imagined. I had started off thinking I was an experienced walker embarking on a comfortable eight-day journey, and it was nothing of the sort. I quickly learned that I was an experienced day walker, but not an experienced long-distance walker. The South Downs Way had been painful and challenging at times, but it had also been magical.

I had hated it at times, but I had also loved it. And now that it was over, I was craving it all over again, despite my aching feet. Part of me wished I could hop on a train to Winchester and start it all over again, pain and all.

Somewhere in those 100 miles, I had fallen in love with the South Downs Way.

EPILOGUE

My experience walking the South Downs Way was wonderful and horrible and also magical. I relished the experience of feeling like I was in another world, somehow separate from ordinary reality yet so close to home. I loved the feeling of carrying everything on my back and of making my way, step by step, toward my end goal of Eastbourne.

The South Downs Way is easily accessible at both ends of the trail, and it's also easy to split it up into day walks or weekend walks, as many people do. It's so close to everything, and yet it's so remote that I felt like I was miles and miles away from civilization. It was that feeling of remoteness that gave it such a magical feel—like I existed in an alternate reality for the eight days I walked the Way.

As I write this, it's been almost a year since I walked the South Downs, and what's funny is that, for the most part, only the positive bits have stayed with me. I remember the good elements: the sunshine, the narrow paths between fields of grain, and the 360-degree views. I have only a vague memory of the painful parts: the aching in my feet, the irritation of my boots pressing my socks against my blisters, and my stiff, aching muscles. My emotional memories are tied to the good bits, and the difficult parts are just factual memories. It's almost as if my brain is conspiring to get me out on another long-distance walk by blocking the hard details from my mind. But then, that happens a lot in life, doesn't it?

My legs were sore for a few days after I returned, and it was only a couple of days before my feet returned to a normal, pain-free state. It felt good to walk around without my heavy pack on my back, and I spent most of my time either barefoot or in sandals in the days after my arrival to let my feet heal. The blisters dried up quickly, and before long, they were gone.

It felt a bit odd to be out in civilization after so many days alone on the Way. People's reactions to my journey ranged from surprise to horror. It seems that a 100-mile walk is something most people would rather avoid. When telling people I walked the South Downs Way from point to point, I usually got the following questions: Did you do it for charity? Did you do it with a group?

The answer to both of those questions is no. I did it for the love of walking, and for that reason alone. I still relish that simplicity of life and the meditative quality of being alone on the trail for hours at a time, to the point where my thoughts fade into the background and are replaced with a deep stillness that is not usually present in my daily life.

After returning from my walk, it was also strange to have so much stuff spread out all over my house, rather than having everything I needed in one place: my backpack. I had gotten used to such a simple, compact lifestyle for those eight days: life was reduced to the things I had in my pack and to the simple act of putting one foot in front of the other for 100 miles.

I enjoyed the feeling of carrying all of my belongings for the week on my back. It felt good to be mostly self-sufficient, though I was staying at B&Bs and eating in restaurants in the evenings. I missed being alone on the trail, dependent on myself every day to make it to each night's destination.

Most importantly, I've since decided that I *am* a long-distance walker.

Reviewing and editing this book made me want to get back on a trail. After quickly researching other trails in Britain, I decided to first walk the Downs Link, a 37-mile (59 km.) flat trail linking the North Downs Way and the South Downs Way. It runs along an old railway line and can be done in three short days of walking. It sounded like a good test: more than a day walk, yet much less than 100 miles.

I walked the Downs Link in May 2016, and it was a fabulous experience. I had the same hot and sunny weather I had experienced on the South Downs Way, meaning I had to carry almost three liters of water each day once again. But it rekindled my love for long-distance walks, and I started planning my next National Trail: the Ridgeway, an 87-mile trail that runs between Avebury and Ivinghoe Beacon.

Part of me is disappointed in myself for choosing an easier, shorter walk than the South Downs. Somehow I feel like I should be striving for a more difficult next walk, like the Camino de Santiago. But I know I'm not up for that yet, for various reasons: I'm just not willing to commit to such a long journey, and I relish the idea of being alone for long periods. I can get that from a National Trail, and I know I won't get that on the Camino.

Plus, there's something enticing about walking another trail in England, where the countryside is so, so gorgeous. It's actually a relief to realize that I *will* be heading out on another long walk. I look forward to long days of meditative walking out in Nature.

As I put together the manuscript for this book, I wondered whether it was actually worthwhile to create a book detailing my experience of the South Downs Way. I have always loved reading stories of other people's walks, but I was concerned that my story was not worth telling. Would people get to the end of the book and regret the time they had invested in reading it?

As if they were aware of my thoughts and doubts, my Akashic Records Keepers sent me the following message via my weekly Akashic records email:

> *"Are you journaling your experiences? We would ask that you do as all of your walks hold TRUTH for other people who are unable to walk because they have fears or restrictions placed on them. Your thoughts are much welcomed, and we are urging you to do this, Holly. This process will help you and get you started on the book that you have inside of you!"*

And that was all I needed to nudge myself back to polishing the manuscript and getting it ready for editing. I hope you've enjoyed it, and I hope that this book has encouraged you to try long-distance walking for yourself, whether it's on the South Downs Way or somewhere else. Walking a long-distance trail is genuinely life-changing.

The South Downs was such a profoundly satisfying and multi-faceted experience for me, entirely unlike anything else I'd ever experienced in my life. Almost a year after my walk, as I read through this manuscript on my final edit, I relived every painful and beautiful detail of my South Downs journey. As I finished the last chapter, I sat in front of my computer with tears rolling down my cheeks. It was truly magical in so many ways.

Happy walking!

Lessons Learned

Plan, plan, plan in advance, to make your walk as enjoyable and pain-free as you possibly can. It is said that suffering is optional, and I could have avoided all pain and suffering by planning even more in advance. I would have enjoyed my South Downs Way walk even more if I had:

- Called for a cab the first day in Exton to get to the B&B at Droxford. That would have saved me that stressful last two miles. Lesson: try to stay as close as possible to the trail. If that's not possible, get a taxi. It's not cheating.
- Not gotten lost for two miles on the second day. Lesson: really pay close attention to all signposts, junctions, and gates. Read the signs, literally!
- Planned a nine-day itinerary instead of an eight-day one, which would have allowed me to stop and enjoy more of the historical sites. Lesson: don't try to be a martyr; there's no shame in planning a longer journey, especially when the longest day is more than halfway into the walk. Or, take a rest day halfway through and see the sights.
- Changed my socks halfway through Day 4, which was a long, hot day. I could have benefited from taking my boots and socks off at *every single* lunch break. Lesson: keep feet cool and fresh by airing them out and even changing socks halfway during the day. I have since developed the tactic of using two pairs of socks for each day of walking. I wear one pair, then take them off at every rest stop and put on the fresh pair before resuming the trail. I keep swapping socks throughout the day.
- Not been forced to make the detour to Bignor Villa

on Day 4. I should have better planned my water for a long day, which I knew would be hot and which I knew had no water taps. Lesson: check the weather and bring more than enough water to avoid detours.

- Done this walk in a different time of year: even a week earlier, it would have been easier. Walking during British Summer Time is good because you get long hours of daylight, but it can get hot during the summer, despite the bad reputation that Britain has for its weather. Lesson: plan to walk a week earlier or later in the year, especially when walking in the southeast. April and September may be good months.

Learn from my mistakes if you can. No two South Downs Ways are the same, and I'm sure that everyone else who walked the same week that I had a very different experience. But the more you read, and the more you plan, the more you can take these details into consideration. In Part IV, you'll find my top tips on how to have a great experience on the Way.

PART II

INTERMISSION

INTERMISSION

When I walked the South Downs Way in 2015, I chose the coastal footpath on my final day from Alfriston to Eastbourne. I was curious as to what I'd miss along the inland route, which is a bridleway, for use by cyclists and horse riders in addition to walkers. Still, I knew I wanted to finish my South Downs experience by walking along the Seven Sisters. I was not disappointed, though my feet were so sore and aching by the final day, I didn't enjoy the walk as much as I might have if I'd begun my walk in Eastbourne, the Eastern point of the South Downs Way.

And so I decided, almost a year after my original South Downs walk, to revisit this final stage. I planned to walk from Eastbourne to Alfriston along the coastal route, which would allow me to experience the same path in the other direction. The following day, I would return from Alfriston to Eastbourne, this time along the inland route.

Day 1

The first day started out totally overcast, with rain in the forecast for the evening. However, I was hoping it wouldn't start until after I had arrived at my destination in Alfriston. I started out at the same place I had finished my walk the year before: alongside the kiosk at the base of the trail. I started walking up the steep, grassy hillside, excited about experiencing this leg of the South Downs with more energy than I had had the previous year.

This last stage of the Way had been a bit confusing the first time I walked it, and it proved to be the same from the other direction. Many trails were crisscrossing the hillside, and it wasn't always clear which of them was the actual South Downs Way. At the peak of one of the hills, I saw a sign indicating a trail that veered off to the left, which didn't look familiar, but I decided to trust it anyway.

Several signs further on indicated that it was, indeed, the Way. It was also not the same way that I had approached Eastbourne the previous year. The narrow trail wound up, down, and around a hill, with views of the sea off to the left. As I came up to the top of the hill, I could see how I had missed the turnoff the previous year: there was no sign indicating that this little side trail was actually the South Downs Way, and so I had just continued straight on down the main path. This has since changed, and now there's a fingerpost sign at the top.

The air was crisp but too warm for a fleece, so I stopped to take it off before heading further. The trail began to ascend once again, and eventually, I passed the Beachy Head Pub at the top, on my right. I had started out at 10:30 in the morning, and there were still very few people on the trail. It seemed that most people were out for a day walk rather than a full South Downs Way experience, which I had found was quite common the previous year on this stretch of the Way.

The path continued to follow the grassy clifftops of the coastline. Though there were plenty of ups and downs on this part of the trail, I hadn't yet technically arrived at the first of the Seven Sisters. I continued up and around the Belle Tout Lighthouse B&B, and as the trail curved around as it approached Birling Gap, I stopped to admire the multicolored columbines in various shades of white, fuchsia, and all shades of purple.

I remembered these landmarks from the previous year. There was the Belle Tout, where I had considered stopping for ice cream but was feeling too achy to stop and then get back up again, and the National Trust cafe at Birling Gap, where I had taken a break for lunch on their busy outside terrace. It was still too early to eat, so I made a quick stop at the toilets (I'm sharing this so you know where you can find toilets along the way—it's either here or nowhere, as there aren't really any large shrubs to hide behind). I continued on up a road lined with a few houses, then through a bush-lined trail before coming back out into the open on the first (or last, depending on how you approach them) of the Seven Sisters.

I walked up towards the memorial pillar, then down and back up again towards the Sarsen Stone, where I sat down to eat the first part of my lunch. I had forgotten how steep some of the slopes were. The moment I settled in to eat, I noticed that the foot traffic had picked up. Small groups of walkers were passing me as I rested. It was past noon, and the peak walking time had clearly begun.

After a quick bite to eat, I headed back down the steep, open rollercoaster path over the sisters. I was on the top of the fifth (counting from west to east), and had three more to go. I was surprised how easy the walk was, compared to the previous year. The upward bits were steep, as were the downward slopes, but as this was my first day of walking, I could see why the trail was so popular. It was a good workout, but not difficult at all. A perfect day hike.

By this point, I could see the inlet at Cuckmere Haven, where the Cuckmere River joined the sea. I eventually approached what I thought was the first of the sisters (I had lost count by this time), but when I got to the top, I found that there was one more. From there, the wide, open path narrowed down into a more traditional trail as it wound down into the valley of the Cuckmere Estuary. The fields were full of ewes grazing placidly with their lambs. None of them seemed to be bothered by the heavy foot traffic coming down the path.

The trail passed through a kissing gate and headed up another large hill, carpeted with buttercups and little white daisies. As I came down the other side of the hill, I could see the information center in Exceat. I headed straight for it, as I wanted to take advantage of the toilets there. The information center was closed for the day, so after a quick rest on a bench, I was up and back on the Way, with just three miles left to my final destination that day in Alfriston. I resolved to slow down and take my time, as I was making much faster progress than I had the previous year.

From here, the trail transformed from open cliffs and fields to a shady wooded trail that I remembered from my first walk through the area. I had passed a few runners heading towards Eastbourne, and now they started to appear in higher numbers: not just runners, but also walkers. I later learned that it was a charity event for diabetes.

Heading down a steep flight of woodland stairs, I emerged in the tiny hamlet of Westdean, where I took another break on a bench alongside a little pond. The day seemed to be going quickly and easily, and I wanted to really enjoy the journey, rather than rush forth to Alfriston. The trail headed uphill once again, winding through the deep shade of Friston Forest.

Coming out the other side of the woods, I was once again in open farmland, on a narrow trail that bordered the left side of the fields and was framed by a thick hedgerow on the other side. The white horse of Litlington was clearly visible off to my left, a white chalk carving that was cut into the hillside sometime in the 19th century, replacing an earlier figure whose origin is unknown.

The Way dropped down into the quiet village of Litlington, where I briefly got lost when I missed a sharp turn off the main street that led down a narrow alleyway (I was distracted by a garden center and tea garden off in the distance). The Way then quickly exited the village to end up on a riverside trail that I recognized from two previous walks I'd done: the Time Out walk from Glynde to Seaford and my first South Downs walk. This was all familiar territory, and I could see the spire of the Alfriston church off in the not so far distance.

After a brief stroll down the flat, easy path near the river, I eventually reached the point where the South Downs Way split into two: the coastal trail that I had walked along on this day, and the inland trail I would take the following day. Here, I crossed the river via a relatively modern bridge and headed straight to Alfriston's High Street, where I would be staying at The Star Inn, which dates back to the 13th century.

Alfriston is perhaps the prettiest little village along the South Downs Way, and it's well worth exploring once you've settled into your accommodation and dropped off your things. If you can plan your walk to leave earlier in the day, so you can arrive early afternoon, then do so. You won't regret it. This also means that you'll want to plan a weekend walk like this as far in advance as possible: Alfriston is very, very popular on weekends and it may be difficult to find accommodation in the village itself.

Day 2

I left Alfriston earlier than planned. I had gone down for breakfast just before nine, thinking I'd have a leisurely meal while reading a book, then check out of the hotel at ten so I could arrive at the local store and pick up a sandwich after it opened. Breakfast was busy, and it didn't make sense to linger with a book, so I went back to my room and packed up my things. After reviewing the highlights of the day's walk, I could see at least a couple of places where I would be able to get lunch along the way. If I didn't manage to pass either of those places around lunchtime, there was always the kiosk at the end of the Way in Eastbourne.

I decided to check out immediately and get started on my walk. After walking out of the village and back across the bridge I had crossed the previous day, I took the turnoff for the inland branch of the Way. It started out much as the coastal route had ended the day before, following closely alongside the River Cuckmere until it made a sharp turn, crossed a quiet country lane, and headed down a shady track that was lined with trees.

It was another dry day, with a hazy cloud-free sky. It was already sunny and hot, and it was looking to be a scorching afternoon. Sun was forecasted all day long.

Coming out of the tree-lined path, the Way crossed another small road and then headed up a hill into farmland. As I walked down the other side of the hill, I realized I was very close to the turnoff to Wilmington, and took out my map to figure out which way to go. The detour headed down the left side of Windover Hill, while the Way wound around the right side of the hill. If I continued on the Way, I'd miss the Long Man entirely, passing just behind him.

The Long Man of Wilmington, a seventy-meter tall chalk figure of a man carved into the hillside, involves a short detour off the Way that is well worth making. The inland leg of the South Downs is significantly shorter than the coastal stretch, and a side trip to see the Long Man helps to round out the day in terms of both cultural interest and length of the journey. As the trail wound around the hillside, I was able to see the Long Man. There was an information board at the foot of the hill.

As my guidebook indicated that the best place to view the Long Man was from the lane leading out of Wilmington village, I took a narrow path that cut through fields to end up on the road leading into Wilmington. I walked up toward the village until I reached a bench alongside the road. Naturally, it was situated at the perfect angle from which to view the Long Man.

After a brief rest to view the chalk figure, I decided to do some more exploring. I had read about some ruins of an old Benedictine priory located in Wilmington, and I eventually found them at the end of a car park. Nothing more than some crumbling walls, I wouldn't say they were worth the detour. But again, this is a short day's walk, so if you're curious, then, by all means, check out the ruins. From there, I retraced my steps back up the hill past the Long Man and then up to the Way. I later calculated that I had added two miles to my walk, making this second day almost precisely as long as the first day's walk.

This inland stretch of the Way is very much like other days on the South Downs: a white chalk trail winding up, down, and around rolling green fields of crops with spectacular views all around. I felt back at home on the Downs. The path continued this way until it entered a shady woodland on its way into the village of Jevington.

The shade was welcome after so much sunshine, and as I approached the village, I passed St. Andrew's Church, where I sat for a few minutes on a shady bench in the churchyard. From there, the Way headed straight down into the village, where I passed the Jevington Tea Rooms, the second option for lunch that day (the first had been in Wilmington, though it had been much too early to eat at that point). I still wasn't hungry, so I walked straight past the tea rooms, peering in between the bushes as I went. It appeared to be a lovely place for tea or lunch; the only problem is that I wasn't at all hungry.

After Jevington, the Way headed steadily uphill and over a grassy hilltop, and then descended the other side. The trail was wide and open, and now that I was approaching Eastbourne (I could see it off in the distance), there were more walkers on the Way. The trail headed down into a golf course and then crossed a road before going back up another hill that looked very much like the final hill on the Way, where I had begun the previous morning.

I could feel the crisp sea breeze, which was very welcome after the hot and sunny day. I knew that this inland bridleway stage of the Way didn't have the same endpoint as the footpath, and by this point, I was hungry and wanted lunch at the kiosk. There were so many trails heading off in all directions, so when the Way took a sharp left turn to head down a hill, I knew I had to keep going toward the coast.

Eventually, I managed to find my way back down to the steep hill that marked the end of the South Downs Way, and I could see the kiosk at the foot of the slope. The short detour to see the Long Man had made this a very decent second day of walking on the South Downs, despite my initial worry that it would end up being too short. It was the perfect weekend loop to revisit the Downs after my through-walk the previous year, and I highly recommend it to anyone looking for a great weekend walk that's easily accessible from London. Also, because this walk consists of two fairly short ten-mile days, you could make it into one long day walk.

PART III

THE PLEASURE

INTRODUCTION

A part of me always knew that I would return to walk the full length of the South Downs Way once again. I first walked the trail in 2015, and I walked the Eastbourne-Alfriston-Eastbourne loop the following year. After that, I revisited bits of the Way for short day walks so I could enjoy some of the things I missed the first time around. I walked the area around The Devil's Jumps so I could visit the field of round barrows, and I walked Old Winchester Hill with my friend Cathy.

I also walked other short- and long-distance trails and wrote books about my experiences: The Ridgeway, the Downs Link, and the Wey-South Path. I planned to walk the Dales Way, but that kept getting postponed for various reasons. And then, in 2019, I decided to update this book and walk the South Downs Way a second time. I felt convinced that I had learned my lessons and that I would be able to enjoy the experience better. You see, while I loved my first South Downs adventure, I don't think that came across in the first edition of this book. There was a lot of pain and blisters, and that seemed to drown out my enjoyment of the whole experience. I wanted to re-walk the trail and prove to myself that it could be different—and also share that experience with my readers.

The second time on the trail *was* easier: much, much easier. I chose to walk the first week of September 2019 when I hoped the weather would be a bit cooler than it had been in June-July 2015. I knew I would be risking more rain, but I had to take the chance. It turned out that the weather was *perfect*: sunny but not hot, and just a bit windy and misty on one day only. I was able to apply everything I had learned in all my previous walking adventures, and I was able to avoid all my big mistakes. As a result, I had a spectacular time on my second South Downs journey. The two experiences were like night and day. It was shockingly different—in a good way.

That's why it's so crucial for me to share my stories from both of my experiences: so you can learn from my mistakes, and so you can learn how great things can be when everything goes right. Planning can make everything easier. Experience can make everything easier. Weight loss can make everything more easier, too.

As with my first South Downs adventure, I pulled one oracle card for each day of the journey. I also pulled an extra card to represent the overarching theme of the walk: Butterfly —Transformation is beautiful. This turned out to be the case with my experience. While my first South Downs walk was full of blisters, sweat, and tears, the second one was full of joy, presence, and wonder. It was very much an emotional experience, whereas the first time around had been very physical. It was glorious. I was so, so thrilled that I had made plans to do the walk again. Please join me now on my adventure ....

DAY 1

WINCHESTER TO EXTON: 12 MILES

Hummingbird–Be Here Now! was the oracle for my first day of walking. It reminded me of the card I had pulled for Day 4 of my first South Downs Way adventure: Delight in the Moment. I resolved to stay present as I walked, and not get caught up in my thoughts. I remembered how irritable I had been on my first day of walking four years prior, and I hoped that state of mind would not repeat itself.

The Morning

I woke up well before either of my two alarms. Tossing and turning for at least a half-hour, I eventually looked at my watch and gave up: I had just thirty or so minutes until my alarm was due to go off. I got up, showered, and reviewed everything I was bringing. Could I get rid of anything? No. Did I need to add anything? Certainly not. I still had clear memories of just how much my feet had suffered on my first South Downs adventure.

One thing I was undecided about: which shoes to wear. You'd think I would have that figured out by now, but I was seriously debating what to do. I generally wear leather hiking boots during winter walks and rainy/muddy walks, but the weather looked too good to wear them this week. For the rest of the three seasons, I usually wear Gore-Tex hiking shoes. But my favorite shoes had given me problems with my Achilles tendons the previous year, and I didn't want to deal with that. I had been reading lots of stories of people preferring to walk in trail running shoes, and I was tempted to give that a try. So I did.

The train journey was uneventful: despite my first train being a bit late, I had no problems at either of my two connections. It was smooth sailing and was a good omen for the long-distance walk I had ahead of me. Before too long, I arrived in Winchester, and I finally felt the full excitement of my journey. I was there. It was real. And I couldn't wait to get started. I headed down the road from the station into the city, turning right and then left through familiar streets.

Since my first South Downs Way adventure in 2015, the official start of the trail had changed from Winchester Cathedral to the City Mill, a small National Trust property that probably goes unnoticed by most of Winchester's visitors. My guidebook suggested that perhaps walkers might want to ignore the new starting point and instead begin at the Cathedral.

I considered that suggestion. Did I want to start at the Cathedral once again? No, I did not. This year, as in 2015, I had no intention of visiting the Cathedral. I was ready to walk the trail.

I had been looking forward to walking the Way again ever since I finished it the first time. Much had changed for me: I had another National Trail under my belt (The Ridgeway), and I had done shorter trails such as the Downs Link and the Wey-South Path several times. I had more experience. And I was in better shape: in both 2017 and 2018, I signed up for —and completed— the Walk 1,000 Miles challenge. I had high hopes that I could return to the South Downs Way and actually enjoy it a little more than I had the first time.

The Walk

The City Mill was easy enough to find. I took a photo of the sign marking the new start of the South Downs Way, and I headed off down an urban path alongside the river. It was a lovely day, and there were plenty of people out for a stroll. I was really enjoying the walk through the riverside gardens, though things started to get confusing at a point where the trail seemed to split. I wasn't sure which way to go, but it looked like both branches met up again at the end of the park, so I picked one and kept going.

When I got to the end of the gardens, I wasn't sure which way to go. No apparent signs were indicating which direction was the way to the South Downs. I turned left, as that seemed to be the way heading out of Winchester. It seemed as though history was repeating itself: I clearly remembered getting lost the previous time, and the signs didn't make it obvious where the Way departed from the riverside. I approached a man who looked like he was kitted up to walk a long-distance trail, and together we found our way out of Winchester. It's funny how paths can be so well marked when you're out in the middle of nowhere, and there aren't many options of where to turn, but when you're in an urban area with so many different possibilities, the trails are a mystery.

Eventually, we got on track, and as we headed up a shady street through the outskirts of Winchester, things started to look familiar. Shortly after crossing the A3, we passed through the threshold of what I personally considered the official start of the trail: the point where the city ended, and Nature began. I remembered having seen a small deer bounding away from me the first time I had been there. On this day, there was no deer.

But it was a Monday morning, not a Saturday as it had been in 2015, and the trail was tranquil. Not a cycle in sight, and just a handful of other walkers. At this point, it was impossible to tell whether they were walking the entire trail in one go, or whether they were just traveling for a day or two. The weather was warm but not hot, and the sky was a bright blue with white fluffy clouds. It appeared to be perfect walking weather.

Richard and I walked together until we reached a water tap in Chilcomb, where he paused to refill his water supplies, and I continued on, eventually passing a small group of walkers with a dog. I carried on for quite some time, recognizing some portions of the trail and walking through others as if it were the first time. There were so many segments of the trail on this first day that I had absolutely no recollection of—it was as though I were walking them for the first time. This was simultaneously unnerving and exciting: was I lost, or was my memory just that terrible?

My first significant discovery of the day: what a difference the seasons make! While last time I had walked in the peak of summer, now the warmer months were transitioning into fall. The air felt crisper in the mornings—and also in the evenings, as I would discover later that day. It seemed to be the perfect time of the year to walk a long-distance trail in England.

The scenery was also different: before, I had walked through unharvested fields of grain, dotted throughout with red poppies. Now, the hedgerows were full of late blackberries, lush and ripe, and still delicious. I snacked on them as I walked. The bright red hawthorn haws were out, and so were the dark purplish-black sloes. Feathery white old man's beard made all the greenery look frothy and fresh.

There were new water taps on the trail that weren't even in my guidebook, and I filled up my water bottle at each of them. I was experimenting with a new hydration system: I planned to use my water reservoir for sipping water as I walked, and I had a one-liter Nalgene bottle for drinking more deeply when I sat down for a break. It was this bottle that I was topping up at each water tap. I had discovered in my day-walks and in my long-distance walks that while a water reservoir was convenient for keeping hydrated little by little with sips of water as I walked along the trail, I ended up not actually drinking very much. My new theory was that I could take in the bulk of my water as I sat for rests, and stay hydrated in between breaks with the water tube. It actually ended up working very well.

My mind kept wandering between the present moment and my previous journey down the trail. Other thoughts and distractions from my daily life intruded into my stream of consciousness. I recalled the day's theme: "Be here now!" and I resolved to stay more present in the moment. I made a little song out of the phrase, which served to remind me of the daily theme. I kept returning to this song throughout the rest of the day.

There were no benches, no places that looked good for taking a break. My energy was flagging, and I really wanted a rest, but I wasn't sure where. And then I crossed a lane and recognized a place where I had stopped for a break on my first trip: a shady, grassy patch alongside the trail. I dropped my pack down and sat beside it. I was long overdue for a break, and I had promised myself that I would take it easy on this trip: if I had learned one thing, it was that taking frequent and short rest stops helped me to walk further in comfort. I was determined to learn from my mistakes on this journey.

After a few minutes, I continued on for another half hour or so, until I realized I needed another break, so I plopped myself down on a grassy stretch alongside a narrow country lane. I pulled out my guidebook and realized that just a few minutes further down the trail, there was a pub I could stop at for a cool drink. This motivated me to get up and go. There were better places to rest!

As I approached, I realized it was the same place I had stopped for a break four years prior. But it was a Monday, not a Saturday, and fortunately, I got to the pub just minutes before it closed at 2pm. I purchased a bottle of cold sparkling water at the bar and took it straight to the garden, where I sat in the shade of an umbrella at a picnic table. I peeled off my shoes and socks to air out my feet. It was time to change to a fresh pair of socks.

As I sat resting, other walkers came to take a break in the pub garden. They were disappointed that it was closed, but they all sat down and pulled out packed lunches. It seemed that there were a few small groups of people and one solo woman who bore a giant backpack full of camping gear. The walkers didn't seem to know each other, but they were all so chatty, and I wasn't feeling particularly social. I realized that this was prime time for me to get up and return to the trail, so I wouldn't get caught walking in a group of people. After finishing my water, I put on my fresh socks, packed up everything, and went off.

Here, the trail followed a quiet country lane for a few minutes before veering off into a shady, tree-lined path that ran parallel to the road. Eventually, the Way met back up with the lane before splitting into two: the trail for walkers went through a gate and into a field, and the trail for cyclists and horse riders went down the road.

The view was gorgeous: a wide, open panoramic vista of the South Downs, with the little village of Exton off in the distance. I remembered stopping here on my first trip, feet in pain, feeling like I couldn't go on much longer. While I wasn't in pain this time, I thought it might be a good idea to have another rest.

A woman came by with her two children, about ages 8 and 9, and paused to say hello. They were walking just the first two days of the trail, but they had farther to go than I did on this first day. They stopped for a rest not far away from me, and we both got up to continue at about the same time.

Here, the trail descended quite steeply in places, and we went through field after field before arriving at one that was full of cattle. The cows were everywhere, and there really wasn't a way to go around them. The woman and her children approached me as we surveyed the situation. There were plenty of cows, but no calves, so it looked reasonably safe. I offered to go through first, and they followed. Unnervingly, the cows didn't make much of an effort to get out of our way, and we had to slowly wind our way through the herd. Soon enough, we were out on the other side of the field, unscathed.

From there, it was smooth sailing through stile after stile until I reached Exton, where I soon found my accommodation for the night at the Manor House. I was tired, and my legs were tired, and my shoulders were tired. But I wasn't in pain like I had been on the first trip. It was indeed a good omen. If today was a snapshot of how the entire week was meant to go, then this week would be a treat. Despite having slept little more than five hours, I had a thoroughly enjoyable first day on the trail.

The Evening

The Manor House is the only accommodation right in Exton. It's got two rooms, but they're within the same building, and the owners only rent out the second room if the occupants know each other, as they share a common area. This was the priciest place I had booked along the trail, but I figured it was worth it to stay right in Exton. I remembered my unfortunate journey the first time I walked the path, and I wanted to avoid that.

The accommodation at the Manor House is spacious and comfortable. There are a large sitting room and kitchen, two bathrooms, and then one or two bedrooms, depending on how many people are in your party. After a quick shower and change of clothes, I put on the kettle and had a bite of the very fresh homemade Victoria sponge that had been left for me on the kitchen counter. While I don't eat very much cake in my day to day life, I always find it particularly satisfying after a long day's walk. And I absolutely love a B&B that provides guests with homemade cake in the room.

My husband had offered to drive me to Winchester that morning, but I suggested that he meet me for dinner in Exton instead. It wasn't far from home, and he could bring me some things that I was missing: when I had packed the night before, I realized that I couldn't find the Bluetooth keyboard that I used for writing on the trail, so I had had to order another one online. Also, I had decided that these particular trail running shoes didn't have a wide enough toe box to be comfortable for long-distance walking, and I wanted to change to my usual hiking shoes.

It ended up being the most lovely dinner at The Shoe Inn. I had thought it would be strange to meet up since I had left my "normal" life and was already fully immersed in that other-worldly feeling of being on the trail. But it was so lovely to have dinner. After the pub, he followed me back to my room at the Manor House, and we exchanged shoes as I set up my new keyboard for my iPad.

When I finally got to bed that night, I was exhausted and thoroughly looking forward to a good night's sleep. Unfortunately, it didn't come as quickly as I anticipated. But when it did come, it was deep and was interrupted only once.

DAY 2

EXTON TO BURITON: 12.5 MILES

Wolf–Turn Knowledge into Wisdom was the card of the day. I certainly liked the sound of that. It gave me the impression that I'd be doing some deep thinking on my walk. Perhaps I'd arrive at some important conclusions about my life and my plans. I was looking forward to this!

The Morning

I reluctantly woke up to my alarm from a profound sleep. I had been startled from my slumber once during the night when I heard someone crunching their way through the gravel drive very near my window, just before 4:30 in the morning. I had looked at my phone to check the time, then I had returned to my deep sleep. I felt rested and refreshed, but I had the tiniest bit of a sore throat, which worried me. I couldn't remember the last time I had had a cold, and I certainly didn't want one now.

However, it had been a long time since I had slept so well: I was using an Oura ring to track my sleep cycles in the hopes of improving my sleep, and lately, things hadn't been going well. I had gotten better at getting to bed earlier, and I was sleeping longer, almost eight hours some nights. But for the previous couple of weeks, my sleep hadn't been profound. One day on the South Downs Way remedied that.

I had a delicious breakfast in the conservatory of the Manor House, and then I wandered through the formal gardens before returning to my room to pack everything up. I went through all the rooms twice to make sure that I wasn't forgetting anything —my biggest fear, since I needed everything I was carrying with me—and then I grabbed my pack and poles, and I was out the door.

The Walk

Weather matters. Weight matters. Rest matters. These were my thoughts as I began the second day of my South Downs journey. The early autumn weather made walking so much easier. I was lucky that it hadn't rained, but I reckoned that even some rain would be preferable to the heat I had walked in the first time around. And since 2015, I had lost some weight, which meant that the burden on my feet was much lighter. That made a huge difference. And getting a good night's sleep meant that I was feeling much more ready to tackle the day than I had the morning before.

I wandered around a bit before finding my way through Exton. The South Downs Way passed right down the little lane right outside the Manor House, yet I didn't remember walking down that road four years ago. I vaguely remembered having walked past The Shoe Inn, though the sign clearly indicated that the walkers' branch of the Way went down the lane I was on. I opened the OS Maps app on my phone and confirmed this before heading more confidently ahead.

Ordnance Survey (OS) is *the* national mapping agency for Great Britain, and they have an excellent series of printed and digital maps, including a phone app that shows you exactly where you are located on the map.

Soon enough, the Way crossed another road and headed into Nature. Things felt right once more...until they didn't. The trail entered a shady line of trees, and then suddenly split into two: a higher, narrow path that snaked through the left-hand side of trees, and a lower, wider trail that looked easier to walk down. I took the low road, keeping my eye on the parallel path to the left to make sure it didn't veer off somewhere. I still wasn't sure which one I was meant to be on. In my experience, two parallel trails often met up further down the line, and it didn't matter which one I took. But I was determined not to get lost.

The upper trail went up some stairs, then down again. My lower trail approached what appeared to be an old railway bridge. I went under it, still eyeing the other path to my left. When I came out on the other side of the tunnel, I realized where I was, and I remembered getting lost in this very place four years prior. I now realized that in 2015, I had taken the trail meant for cyclists and had ended up right at this bridge, not knowing where to go. The only difference between then and now was that the lower trail had been cleared, whereas before it had been overgrown and impossible to walk through.

I saw a sign indicating which way to go, and all was clear. When I had left that morning, the day had been overcast and gray, looking like it might rain any moment. But in the short time that I had been walking—maybe a half-hour—it had cleared up, and the sun was out. It was another perfect day for walking: warm but not hot, with a slight breeze. I was so pleased with my decision to walk in early September.

The trail steadily climbed as it approached Old Winchester Hill, the Iron Age hill fort. There were expansive views all around of golden and green farmland. I remembered the pretty blue fields of flax I had seen in 2015. Now everything was green.

At a point where the trail turned a sharp right to go around a field, I passed the woman I had seen the day before with the huge backpack. She was sitting down, enjoying a break. We greeted each other, and I continued on. I never saw her again on the trail.

I passed signs for Old Winchester Hill and ignored them. I had just been there two weeks prior, walking with a friend. Here, the Way was well signposted, and as it turned away from the hillfort, there was a clear sign splitting it into two: cyclists and horse riders on the lower trail, walkers, and wheelchairs— wheelchairs?!—on the higher path. I couldn't imagine how a wheelchair could possibly navigate the trail, even though it was relatively wide and smooth, but then I saw two women coming toward me with a baby stroller for twins. It clearly was an all-access trail.

I sat down on a bench to rest, and a group of about six older walkers passed me. This was the first time I had crossed paths with them, and I did not know it at this time, but I would see them at least once every day until the end of my journey. We greeted each other, and they stopped at a bench further on. I had resolved to take it easy and rest often: I was in no rush to get to my destination. I reminded myself of what my scuba instructors used to say: "Clear your ears early and often," except I was going to apply this concept to my walking: "stop and rest early and often" would be my motto for this week.

My daily theme—Turn Knowledge into Wisdom—kept slipping into my mind throughout the day. As I walked, I got an idea for a couple of online community projects related to my work that I planned out in my head: one mindset-related and another Nature- or channeling-related. I kept turning the ideas over and over in my head as I walked. Was *this* the knowledge I was meant to turn into wisdom? Or was it something else? Was I expected to be incorporating the knowledge I had gained from my previous walking experience into something? Who knew? I walked on.

Shortly after, I approached Meon Springs, where I stopped for yet another break. I made myself a mug of hot tea inside the cabin and sat down at the table. I had only been there twice before on my walks, but I had never seen the place so busy. It turned out that they had their regular fishermen there, plus a corporate group, and also a charity event. Fortunately, most people were outside, and it was relatively quiet inside the little cabin. I asked to fill up my water bottle in the kitchen, and then I was off, though, as I returned to the path, I noticed a new water tap right on the trail that hadn't been there four years prior. Hydration facilities had undoubtedly improved.

The trail was an open, stony track with no shade as it passed in between fields, climbing gently. I reached the top of the slope, and the trail turned right, passing now through a leafy green tunnel of trees. It began to climb once more, steadily, still in the shade. The path turned into a holloway: a sunken trail between the tree-lined banks on either side. Eventually, the trail came out onto a quiet country lane and continued ahead, sloping uphill. I stopped for a rest, sitting on a grassy spot alongside the road. There was not a car in sight. I pulled out my guidebook and realized that I was very close to The Sustainability Centre, where I had planned to take a break, so I got up and continued my journey.

The Sustainability Centre offers camping, yurts, hostel rooms, and a small cafe. I dropped my pack off at a picnic table and went inside to get something cold to drink. What I wanted was sparkling water—something cold and refreshing, but without sugar—but the not so friendly man behind the counter indicated that I could get water from the tap outside. I got a ginger beer instead. Returning to the table outside, I took off my shoes and socks to rest my feet. Looking at my guidebook, it

appeared that I was about halfway through my day's walk, and I
was still feeling pretty good.

I slowly finished my drink, changed my socks, and felt
instantly better. On my way out of The Sustainability Centre, I
passed the group of three couples on their way in. From here,
the Way was somewhat shady, a straight run for about 45
minutes until it passed a farm and turned left down a quiet
road that led to Butser Hill, the highest point on the South
Downs and the site of my next rest stop, with a snack bar and
toilets. I passed a family on their cycles, taking a break. Further
on, I passed two walkers sitting alongside the trail. It had been
a tranquil day on the path, but then it was a weekday, so that
wasn't surprising. The trail was just as I liked it.

When I reached Butser Hill, I immediately saw that both
the snack bar and the toilets were closed, but there were plenty
of picnic tables outside to rest on. I took my shoes off and aired
out my feet as I leisurely watched a group of people flying
model airplanes nearby. Once my feet were thoroughly dry, I
tended to a blister between two of my toes, changed my socks
once more, and headed off toward the Queen Elizabeth
Country Park, my next stopping point. In my effort to "stop and
rest early and often," I realized that I had unconsciously split
this day's walk into mini-stages. There were so many obvious
places to rest on this day, unlike the previous one.

From here, the trail headed gently downward, on an open,
grassy hill dotted with small trees and shrubs. The A3 loomed
noisily ahead of me, the landmark that indicated the last bit of
my walk through the Queen Elizabeth Country Park. The trail
descended a bit more steeply as it approached the bottom of
the hill. Here, the Way passed under the A3 and came out the
other side near the car park, which led to the visitor center and
cafe, which I could see was under construction. This was disap-
pointing, as I had planned to have a very late lunch here: my
accommodation at Nursted Farm was a mile and a half outside

Buriton village, and I had no intention of walking back into Buriton for dinner that evening.

Fortunately, there was a temporary cafe set up in a marquee on the lawn, and I sat down for my final rest of the day and a late lunch. It was simple food: I ordered a cheeseburger and a bag of crisps, and I settled in at a picnic table to eat. I took off my shoes as I waited for my food to arrive. I had been hoping that the frequent airing of my feet would keep them blister-free. Since I had already developed my first blister of the week, I contented myself with the idea that I would at least be limiting the total number of blisters I might develop this week. It worked.

Once I had finished my meal, I hoisted my pack on my back and continued. I remembered very clearly just how tired I had been on this day, four years, and two months earlier. I remember my aching feet and legs, and how badly I just wanted to arrive. In contrast, on this day, my feet and legs were tired, yes, but they were doing pretty well. I carried on, picking up the South Downs Way, and walking steadily into the woods.

I crossed paths with a woman on her own who was also going to Buriton and asked for directions. I explained how she could get there by following the South Downs Way. She turned around and followed me as I climbed the trail up the final hill of the day. Her foot was injured, so it would be slow going for her. Fortunately, she was staying in the village and not at the farm, so she had a shorter journey than I did.

About a half-hour later coming down the other side of the hill and out from the forest, I saw a sign indicating Buriton to the left, down the road. There were trails heading the same direction straight in front of me, and the South Downs Way carried on to my right. I remembered having taken the road on my previous visit, so I pulled out my OS Maps app to see where the trail went. It was actually a path called Hangers Way, and it went straight into Buriton. I later learned that Hangers Way is a

20.4 mile, or 32.9 km trail that begins at Alton Rail Station and finishes at the Queen Elizabeth Country Park, where I picked it up. The trail passes along a series of steep, wooded hills, which are known as "The Hangers."

I opted to take Hangers Way and continued ahead. The trail went straight through the site of the old Buriton chalk pits—a local nature preserve—with the pits themselves somewhere off to the right of the path. Apparently, chalk has been quarried from the South Downs for hundreds of years, which is not surprising considering the chalky white trails that make up much of the South Downs Way. It is believed that large-scale quarrying began in Buriton with an established lime works in about 1860. Many of the paths around the old chalk pits follow the old narrow-gauge railway lines that were used to move the chalk and lime around the site.

Hangers Way was shady, and the soft dirt trail made for easy walking. Eventually, it headed downhill and came out onto a little road that passed a thatched roof cottage. I knew I was close to the village, and I soon rounded a bend and arrived at the small pond in front of the Church of St Mary in Buriton.

I was still feeling good, but I knew I had another mile and a half of street walking to go, so I sat down on a bench for yet another rest while I consulted my map to make sure I headed down the correct lane to get to my accommodation. Once that was confirmed, I headed off down North Lane. At one point, a footpath appeared off to my right, parallel to the road. I consulted my map, satisfied my question that it would still bring me to my destination, and took it. A dirt footpath was much easier on the body than the hard asphalt of a road, and it was a lot less stressful since I didn't have to worry about cars.

The footpath eventually came back out onto the road, so there was more asphalt walking for the last bit of my journey. Before long, I saw the sign for Nursted Farm and happily turned up the drive. As I rang the doorbell of the old farmhouse, I was pleased that I was in much better shape than I had been four years earlier. Tired, and ready for a cup of tea, but in pretty good shape. It must have been all those rest stops!

The Evening

It was a quiet, uneventful evening at Nursted Farm. I was given a different room: a large one with two beds, a sofa, and a spacious en suite bathroom with a bathtub. Everything was immaculate, but dated, like someone's grandparents' house. It only added to the charm of the old farmhouse.

I remembered how lovely it had been to have tea with the other walkers four years prior, but it seemed that I was the only one who had arrived, so a tea tray was brought up to my room for me. There would be another walker staying that night, but apparently, he would be arriving later that evening. And so I settled in for a bath before washing my clothes and resting on one of the beds. I used the dressing table as a desk to write up this day's chapter.

By now, my almost sore throat from the morning had advanced into a full-on cold, and I was sniffling and coughing a bit. I went to bed early, with a handful of tissues, and slept a restless night full of sneezes and sniffles. It seemed that all the poor sleep that had led up to my South Downs walk had resulted in a weakened immune system. I never had more than one cold a year, and it seemed this would be my annual illness.

DAY 3
BURITON TO COCKING: 11+3/4 MILES (18+1.2 KM)

G iraffe–See the Big Picture was the oracle of the day. Once again, I was curious as to how this would play out. What was the big picture that I'd be seeing? Or was this a sign that I wasn't seeing the big picture of something? Only time would tell.

The Morning

As predicted, it had rained overnight, and the morning was still dark and overcast. It looked like it was going to rain all day, despite the weather forecast that proclaimed sunshine. But in the hour it took me to eat breakfast (the other guest was Richard, whom I had met on the first day in Winchester, so we had two days of walking to catch up on) the weather had cleared up beautifully, and I changed from walking trousers into shorts before setting off.

Once again, there was a debate on how to get back to the South Downs Way. I was at least two miles off the trail, and I had several options on how to get back to it, the most obvious one being to retrace my steps from the previous afternoon. But

I didn't want to do that: it would involve another lengthy journey down the lane, only to pick up the Way just where it also went down a country road. At the same time, I didn't want to miss any of the trail.

Richard and I pored over our maps after breakfast, wondering which way we should take. I finally decided what I would do, and I showed him my plan. He agreed that it looked like a good choice and opted to do the same. I planned to start out before he would, but I figured that with all my rest stops, we'd cross paths at some point along the trail.

I had been disappointed that I hadn't seen the farm's owners, Mary and Gordon, but on my out the door, I crossed paths with Mary. I told her how pleased I was to return to the farm, and how much I was enjoying the trail this second time around. I wanted to ask after Gordon, but as Mary herself was in her 80s, I was afraid of the answer, so I thought it best to pretend that all was the same as it had been four years prior. I went out the door without inquiring as to his wellbeing, blissful in my ignorance.

The Walk

I opted to walk part of the way back toward Buriton and then take the Milky Way, a byway that would lead me straight to the South Downs Way. The Milky Way is the name given to a steep path that cuts a diagonal line across the slope of the Downs, taking you down to Buriton—or up from Buriton back to the South Downs Way—through Cockshot Wood. The Milky Way gets its name from the milky white chalkiness of the path, as you might imagine. So many of the trails that connect to the South Downs are just as chalky as the Way itself.

I suspected this might be the very same trail I had taken on my last journey when Mary from Nursted Farm had driven us all back to the path. As soon as I turned off Pitcroft Lane onto the byway, I recognized that it was indeed the same trail. And it was much prettier than I had remembered: lush and green, shady and damp from the night rain. It was a lovely start to the walk, and it was much more beautiful than walking down North Lane back to Buriton. I was pleased with my decision.

About halfway back to the Way, I looked off to my right and saw the church tower off in the distance. I consulted my map and saw that there was a footpath that would take me back to Buriton. From there, I could retrace my steps from the day before. But did I really want to walk a mile on the road? I opted once more to continue down the byway.

The day's theme was: "See the big picture." Was this what I was meant to see— that it was more important to enjoy the journey than to walk every step of the official trail? Was I expected to understand that I was there simply to walk, and to get out in Nature and that choosing a green byway over an asphalt road was in no way cheating? I pondered this as I turned left off the byway onto the official South Downs Way, which was still a paved road at this point.

The quiet country lane led to some farms, and it was lined first with lush green beech trees and further on with copper beeches. I remembered them from my first walk down this lane. Turning left off the road onto a track, I saw the group of three couples I had crossed paths with on the day before. We greeted each other, remarked on how lovely the weather was, and I continued onward.

The track was open and sunny, then fairly wooded and shady. The Way crossed a busy B road, then headed uphill into Harting Downs. A car park was off to the right, and I saw a bench to my left—the first of the day. I headed off the trail and sat my pack down on the bench to rest. I had been walking for about an hour and a half by that point, and I planned to continue my protocol of resting early and often. It seemed to be working well for me.

After several minutes, I stood up to stretch, saw the small group of walkers come out into the clearing, and I decided to continue onward and leave the bench for them. It would be the last time I would see them—or any other South Downs Way walkers—that quiet Wednesday afternoon. The trail was white and chalky, surrounded by a grassy hillside to my right, and exceptional views of patchwork farmland to my left. It finally felt like I was on the South Downs: it was that typical scenery that I so associated with the Way. After a few minutes of this, the trail entered a wooded area and then came out just before Beacon Hill, which I remembered from my first time here. There was a huge walking group of about twenty people waiting by a fingerpost sign at the base of the hill. Here, I had to decide whether to heed my guidebook's suggestion to go up and over the hill—"more fun than the official route to the south"—or continue on the actual South Downs Way.

I remembered having thought that Beacon Hill wasn't actually much fun, though there were great views from the top of it. I had returned to this area after my first South Downs Way adventure when I visited The Devil's Jumps and had taken the official trail to the south of the hill, so I decided to go with this option once more. I had already cut my walk short in the morning; there was no need to do so again. I was in no rush to reach Cocking that afternoon: I wouldn't be able to check into my B&B until 4:30.

I turned right, following the official Way all around the base of Beacon Hill. The trail started out open and sunny, and then it became more wooded and shady. As I neared the tip of the hill, there were sheep grazing in a golden field to my left. The color of the pasture contrasted beautifully against the blue, almost cloudless sky. I paused to take a photo and then continued onward.

My original plan had been to keep going until The Devil's Jumps, a field of round barrows just off the Way, but they seemed to be further than I remembered. The trail turned left, continuing around Beacon Hill until I came to the point where I would have reconnected with the Way had I gone straight over the top. Here, the path turned right and once again had that pure South Downs vibe to it: a broad, chalky white trail on the top of a grassy ridge, with fields all around.

Before long, the path entered a forest once again, then came out into the open. I knew that The Devil's Jumps wasn't too far away, but I wanted another rest, so I dropped my pack onto a grassy bit alongside the trail, and I sat down to have a snack. Two young women walked by with their dogs, and they continued back toward Harting Downs. After several minutes, I stood back up and went on. My legs and feet were tired, serving as a reminder to rest early and often along the trail, but I had none of the aches and pains that I had suffered on my first journey. All was still well!

The trail seemed endless, though I knew I was approaching my next stop. I wasn't in a hurry, but I had such little sense of the distance between points. I remembered some things being so much closer together. Finally, the trail turned left, and I saw the memorial to Joseph Ostermann, the German soldier shot down in 1940. It was adorned with red poppies and a big poppy wreath. Just a few steps beyond was the entrance to The Devil's Jumps.

I turned off the trail, went through the gate, and walked past the first four round barrows until I reached the final tumulus at the end of the field. There, I climbed to the top of the barrow, dropped my pack on the ground, and sat down. I peeled off my shoes and socks to air my feet. The site was open and unprotected by trees, and it was quite breezy. I sat for some time before deciding to find a more peaceful place to rest. I got up and wandered through the site, looking for someplace to relax out of the wind. There was nowhere, not even a deep ditch between two of the barrows.

Since I couldn't find an ideal resting spot at the site, I resolved to continue my journey, and I saw a lone man eating his lunch on the third barrow. We waved to each other, and I headed out of the site and back on the trail. I checked my watch: at the rate I was going, I would arrive at Cocking well before my check-in time. I decided to make multiple lengthy rests before I got there.

The Way went through a shady wooded area, then came out back into the open for the final stretch into Cocking. The track was straight and wide, passing in between fenced off fields on either side. There were no other walkers in sight. I was reminded of my daily theme, and since there was no one else around, I started singing it:

"See the big picture
See the big picture..."

As you can see, I'm a very creative songwriter. Thankfully, I've dedicated my writing to books and blog posts, not music. Usually, all I needed was to repeat the phrase of my theme to get myself focusing on it. But then I surprised myself by continuing:

"And that picture is you."

Ah, so the big picture that I was meant to see today was myself? The words had popped out of my mouth without any thought. I pondered on this as I continued singing. I had been thinking earlier that day of my writing and where I wanted to go with my next books, so that made sense.

Eventually, I could see what appeared to be the two farms near Cocking off in the distance. It was quite early, and it looked that I'd be there by 3pm at the rate I was going. There was really nowhere to rest—there was just a narrow grassy strip between the trail and the fence on each side— but I found a bit that looked like it might be comfortable, and I sat down, taking a load off my feet, but not even bothering to take off my pack. I just leaned back to get the weight off my shoulders a little. It wasn't the best rest stop, but it was a break, and it was an excellent way to pass the time and extend my journey.

I got up and continued walking. I returned to singing my daily theme as I went. Still no one in sight. I passed a giant ball of chalk on my right, another sign that I was approaching Cocking, and then I went gently down what was now a farm track as I got closer to my turnoff. I passed a farmhouse on my left, with two ponies in its yard—one white, one black—and then I turned left at the byway just beyond it.

The trail was relatively narrow and looked more like a footpath than a byway, bordered on both sides by tall hedgerows. It led gently downhill, getting chalkier and more slippery as it neared the bottom, where it came out on the road and turned right. To the right of the lane was a lush green hillside, covered with ferns. It looked like there was a small pond at the bottom of it. I continued past houses until I reached the main road and went straight to the B&B, where I checked the front and back doors before being told by a workman that the owners were out. I went back to the garden and waited at a picnic table for them to arrive and let me in.

The Evening

I didn't have to wait long. Within half an hour, I saw a woman look out the window and motion for me to head around to the back door. I did and took off my shoes as I entered the tea room. She led me up to the same little single room I had stayed in four years prior. I showered, then settled into the room, and waited for dinner.

The main difference between my 2015 stay in Cocking and

my 2019 stay was that the local pub had closed, which meant that the only place for dinner in the village was my B&B. When I went down for dinner, I saw that they had set up one big table for the four of us: two women, who were staying at Moonlight Cottage, and a man who was staying up the road at a farm that offered accommodation. When they arrived for dinner, it turned out that I already knew two of the three. One of the women I had met on the trail on Day 2 just outside Buriton and the man was, of course, Richard.

It was so lovely to have dinner with the three of them. It satisfied my need for interaction with other trail walkers that I had missed when I had tea alone in my room at Nursted Farm. It turned out that the two women were originally from California, though one of them now lived in Alaska. We would cross paths once more on the trail—the following evening—and I grew to think of them as "the California sisters." It was almost dark by the time we finished our meal, and the three of us who were staying at Moonlight Cottage headed up to our rooms, as Richard prepared to walk the mile or so back up to the South Downs Way, where he was staying at a farm.

DAY 4

COCKING TO AMBERLEY: 12 MILES (19 KM)

Peacock:–Let it shine! was the day's theme. It sounded like fun. I wasn't sure what would be in store for me, but I liked the idea of it. At least it wasn't worrisome, like some of the other oracles for the week. Let it shine!

The Morning

I had a leisurely breakfast with the California sisters who, as it turned out, recognized my name as they had read the first edition of this book. I was so pleased to meet someone on the trail who had read my book, but I cringed inside as I wondered what they thought of me. I had had such a rough time on my first South Downs journey, and I had bared my pain with the world in the form of this book. What did they think of me?

Ugh. That old worry again. I was always wondering what people thought of me: were they secretly criticizing me for my weakness? Did they hate the book, despite telling me otherwise? Once more, I felt vulnerable for having shared my story so openly. Yes, I was pleased to meet my readers, but at the same time, the meeting had triggered my insecurities.

It wasn't until months later that I became fully aware of the irony that my present-day worries were so inconsistent with the day's theme: let it shine (like a peacock). I had let myself shine when I first wrote this book, but all that did was trigger the ages-old insecurity that I wasn't good enough. I had done loads of personal development and mindset work over the years, but it seemed that I still hadn't been able to shake this fear. It was getting better, but it wasn't gone completely.

The Walk

After breakfast, I packed everything up in my backpack and went downstairs to settle my bill, collect the sandwich I had ordered, and leave. I crossed paths with an Australian couple I had never seen before as I approached the byway that led up to the South Downs Way. They had been about to take a different trail up and were questioning which one to choose. The byway I planned to take looked more direct, and they followed me up the trail. As the sunken path climbed steadily, I wondered how on earth Richard managed to navigate the trail in the twilight after dinner the previous evening. The days were getting shorter and shorter; fall was clearly approaching.

After what felt like a very lengthy return to the trail, I reached the Way and turned left. This day's segment of the path felt very typical of the South Downs: the white chalk trail cutting through golden fields, alternating with shady green paths through small woodlands. This was also a section that felt very remote: there were no cafes, no farm shops, no fishing centers to get a drink, or a snack. Just a couple of road crossings and a reasonably straight path that led eastward toward Amberley, a pretty little village that I had been through several times before on my walks. Several day-walks that I had done ended there, and the Wey-South Path also finished in Amberley.

And once more, there were no benches to rest on. I remained focused on resting early and often, and I kept my eye on my watch. After I had been walking just over an hour, I sat down alongside the trail in a grassy bit to rest. An hour later, I did the same. At one point, I caught up to the group of three couples who, I found out, were from up north, on the east coast. I passed them when they paused and continued onward. We ended up leapfrogging each other at different points throughout the day, with them passing me on my breaks and me doing the same when they stopped.

Some parts of the trail were very familiar to me; many were not. Once again, I was shocked by how much of the path I had forgotten. On one of my rest stops, I pulled out my list of daily themes and found the one for this day: "Let it shine!" As always, I tried to find the appropriate song for the phrase. It started out like "Let it Go" from Frozen and somehow morphed into "Stayin' Alive" from the Bee Gees, all the time with "Let it shine!" as the lyrics. I'll leave you to imagine how that monstrosity sounded.

After much on-and-off singing of my daily theme, I never figured out what it meant—until, as I mentioned earlier, I re-read this chapter months later as I was working on it. I saw the irony in the morning's conversation as it related to the day's theme of "let it shine." Shining is not something I'm usually good at, so at the time, I figured it was clearly a call for me to do more of that...without feeling the shame and insecurity that I felt from sharing my story.

As the trail entered a more wooded area, I saw signs for Graffham Down. The mostly flat path was lined with yews and beeches and other native trees. It was lush and shady and green. The Graffham Down Trust is an organization that is attempting to re-establish a mixed environment of grassland connected woodland and scrub in an area of about ten acres, or four hectares. Graffham Down Trust is made up of six wildlife reserves: Bowley's Field, Long Meadow, Scott's Corner, Paterson, Parish A (the primary archaeological site, home to a bell barrow, and a bowl barrow), and Dimmer.

Two men on cycles approached me, pausing as they passed. They asked if I were walking the whole trail and if I were carrying all my things with me as I walked. One of them indicated my socks that were hanging off my pack to dry. "We could smell you coming from a mile away!" he said. We all laughed, and I assured him that they were clean. Did people think I was simply airing my dirty laundry, rather than washing it every day? I was slightly horrified by the thought. They continued onward and soon disappeared off in the distance.

The trail emerged out into vast open fields once more, and I clearly remembered this portion of the trail. The sun was shining, and there was a light breeze, making this yet another day of perfect weather for walking. The last time I had been through these fields, they had been full of grain. Today, they were cut short, already harvested. The path sloped gently downward, reminding me that it would soon rise up again on the next hill.

I came out onto a quiet road, which I crossed quickly before heading up the path on the other side. I vaguely remembered a long and steady rise up the hill, so I stopped for another rest. I had just passed a fingerpost sign that indicated that I had passed the halfway point for the day, and I didn't want to arrive too early.

A lone walker I hadn't seen before passed me, and we greeted each other. The group of six also passed me by. I decided to get up and continue on; my guidebook indicated a bench not too far away, and I planned to rest there, also. The Way rose gently and steadily, climbing between trees that shaded the trail. It seemed to take forever to reach the promised bench, which I remembered from my previous walk. It was located just by the first turnoff to Gumber Bothy, a campsite, and bunkhouse where I had camped once the last year.

When I arrived, I put down my pack and took off my shoes and socks, aware that I hadn't yet aired my feet out for the day. I put them up on the bench, waiting for them to dry. So far, my system was working: I had just that one blister between my two toes on my left foot, but I had no idea how to cushion it or prevent it from getting worse other than to keep my feet as dry as possible. I took my time airing them out.

Just about the time that I was thinking about getting on my way, the Australian couple from that morning in Cocking showed up, and I offered them the bench. They were so few and far between that you really had to take advantage of them when you came across them. The way I saw it, this also meant sharing them with other walkers. I put my fresh socks on and went on my way, entering the Slindon Estate, a National Trust property comprised of 3459 acres or 1,400 hectares of woodland, downland, farmland, and parkland. The South Downs Way crosses through some of its farmland: here, the trail was open and unprotected by foliage, running between fields of sheep. The ewes were happily grazing, unbothered by my passing alongside them since I was on the other side of the fence.

I passed the second turnoff to Gumber Bothy, which I remembered fondly as a quiet and remote campground, then I approached the turnoff to Bignor Villa, the detour I had taken to get water on my first walk. There would be no detour for me on this day, as I had plenty of water with me. A new bench had been carved from a tree trunk and was sitting next to the information board. This was the second of only two benches on this stretch of the Way.

The trail continued through golden fields that had already been harvested. Huge tractors rolled speedily through the fields, each carrying one bale of hay, which they deposited on a precariously tall stack of bales before speeding off for the next one. I was happy to be walking on the other side of the fence and not on a footpath that went through the field itself. The farmland seemed endless, but after the trail crossed a busy road, the path was lined with trees on the left side. A mechanic's van lumbered down the byway toward me, and I stepped out of its way so it could pass.

The view opened up once more, and I could see a small village down in the valley to the right of the trail, which according to my map, might be Houghton. I strained my eyes, trying to see Amberley Castle, but nothing was visible. I remembered having done several walks where I could see it off in the distance, and assumed it must have been the Wey-South Path that gave me views of the castle, not the South Downs Way. I could see the trains slowing in the distance as they arrived at Amberley Station, but I still couldn't see where the village was, and I knew the village itself was a bit further on from the station.

Once I reached the flat fields of the valley near Amberley, I stopped for a rest, the last of the day. I could see the group of six far off in the distance. I had passed them at one point as they stopped for lunch. I ate half of my sandwich and then got up to continue my journey. I estimated I had just a half-hour left to go. It seemed as though the day had passed very quickly.

I crossed the bridge over the River Arun, then continued alongside fields and past a water treatment plant before reaching the busy B2139 road. Here, there were two options: turn left, as I had on my previous journey, and go straight into the village, or continue on the South Downs Way and take a turnoff further on. I decided to be a purist and stay on the official trail. I crossed the main road and headed up another smaller road, walking past some houses on a boring asphalt lane. I had walked here before and was regretting my decision as I steadily walked uphill, but at this point, to turn back would have taken me as long as it would to continue forward. And so I went on.

Once I saw the sign for the Wey-South Path where I needed to turn left, I saw that it descended steadily back downhill toward the busy B2139 road once more. I realized that I wouldn't even be saving myself a hill the following morning; I'd simply have to walk up this road again. Arriving back at the busy road, I crossed it once more, this time without too much difficulty. I continued into the village.

I stopped at the village store to get something for my runny nose and cold and ran into one of the California sisters. We crossed paths again just a few minutes later on our way to our respective B&Bs for the night. They were staying right next door to The Sportsman, where I had booked. It was probably the furthest B&B from the trail, but it had accommodation and food, so it seemed like a good option. I remembered enjoying my dinner there on my first South Downs journey.

My arrival at The Sportsman came soon enough, though I saw that it was closed. A sign on the door indicated that I needed to phone someone to be let in, and so I did. Within seconds, it seemed, the door was open, and I was shown to my room, a small but nicely furnished en suite that overlooked the quiet road. I was pleased to see that the room also had a large fan, so after showering and washing my clothes, I set them up to be dried by the fan as I went down to have a drink before dinner.

The Evening

By the time I headed downstairs, the pub was filling up with people. I ordered a pint of Guinness at the bar and headed out to the deck outside to write up this chapter. The view of the Amberley Wildbrooks was spectacular: 202 acres (82 hectares) of wetland habitat that's comprised of a series of man-made ditches that were primarily dug in the 1800s. Over half of the aquatic plants found in Britain grow here. The Wey-South Path winds its way through the wild brooks as it comes into Amberley, so I was well familiar with this land at ground level, but I had never seen it from above. The Sportsman clearly knows what a spectacular view it has, and the owners provide binoculars for its patrons to enjoy it with.

After finishing my pint, I headed back inside and grabbed the same little table where I had eaten four years before. As I settled in, I looked up and saw the other California sister having dinner. I went over to say hello, and she invited me to eat with her, so I grabbed my things from the other table and sat down. Once again, it was so lovely to have dinner with a fellow trail mate. We talked of that day's segment of the trail, and all the other walking adventures we'd had. I realized that while I enjoyed solitude on the trail, it was really satisfying to share a meal with another walker in the evening.

We said goodnight, and that was the last time I saw either of them. The California sisters had a rest day planned further on in Lewes, and our paths never again crossed. I suspected the same might happen with Richard, who also had a rest day planned near Amberley.

DAY 5

AMBERLEY TO BRAMBER: 10 MILES (16 KM)

Ant–Time to Collaborate was the daily oracle. Would I have to collaborate with other walkers? Was this a sign for me to think of collaborations for the future? It seemed like a strange theme for a day of walking, but I was learning that sometimes the oracle wasn't about what would be happening that day, but rather what I would be thinking about.

The Morning

As much as I love a cooked breakfast, I had opted for the continental breakfast at The Sportsman. I couldn't bear the thought of eating sausage and bacon for the fourth day in a row, so I went with what was essentially a carbohydrate fest instead. Because I usually follow a high fat, low carb way of eating, I thought I'd be starving and suffer a carbohydrate crash just a couple of hours later, but I was willing to take the risk. Thankfully, that didn't happen.

Packing up and getting ready to go was easy, mostly because I had managed to thoroughly dry all of my clothes with the fan, which meant that for once, I could pack everything away and not have to worry about it drying. I went downstairs, checked out, and saw a massive group of walkers just outside the pub. I greeted them but was secretly horrified because it looked like it would be a busy day on the trail. Thankfully, they were lingering, waiting for something or someone, and I never saw them again. I wondered if they were the same large group I had seen just before Beacon Hill on Harting Down on the third day.

It was early: only 9:15 when I set out, walking down the lane back toward the village. I decided to take a detour to visit the old church in Amberley. I had been through this village several times now, but as my walking trails always seemed to end here, I never had the energy to stop in to see the church.

St Michael's Church in Amberley dates back to the mid 12th Century, with a south aisle and eastern chancel of about 1230, and a later tower that dates to the 13th Century. It's pretty, but I wouldn't say it was well worth the detour. However, my curiosity was satisfied, and I was pleased that I had made the decision to stop in. From there, I backtracked my way through the village, retracing my steps from the previous day, until I reached the same point where I had come off the trail in the afternoon. At this point, it was just before 10am, so I was still getting an early start to the day.

The Walk

The first stretch of the trail was quite steep by South Downs Way standards, which I didn't remember from my previous journey. Soon enough, I was up on the top of a ridge, with open views to both sides. There were fields to my left, and fields to my right, with the sea beyond them, off in the distance. This was another day of exceptional views all around.

At breakfast, I had debated whether or not it would rain with the two couples with the dog I had first seen just outside of Chilcomb on Day 1. This was the first time I had crossed paths with them since the first day of walking. The sky was completely overcast, full of dark rainclouds, yet the forecast said nothing of rain, and I was confident that we'd be fine. We were: though I felt a couple of random drops of rain at two or three points throughout the afternoon, it was nothing more than that. It still looked as though I would have a rain-free journey.

This was a quiet day on the trail, with no cafes, snack bars, or facilities aside from a water tap about halfway through. It was also a quiet day in terms of people: I passed the two Australians I had seen on and off throughout the week, but I didn't see any of the other walkers that I knew. The group of three northern couples were nowhere in sight, Richard was back in Houghton having a rest day near Amberley, and the California sisters were probably behind me somewhere. I hadn't seen the lone woman with camping gear since the morning of Day 2. It saddened me to think that I wouldn't see some of these people again. I really enjoyed crossing paths with them on the trail, even though we didn't converse much.

At one point, a lone jogger passed me. I saw a few random dog walkers at various locations throughout the day. One woman asked me if I were doing the whole South Downs Way, and when I said yes, she said, "Great! That's the third girl on the trail." I wondered who the other "girls" were since she was coming from the opposite direction. In the second half of the day, there were a few cyclists, passing me by alone or in pairs. They were always so silent as they came up behind me, and they never seemed to use their bells, but for some reason, my fear of cyclists had disappeared, and I was completely unbothered by them. I often remembered my former irritation at silent cyclists and cringed silently to myself.

There were turnoffs on the left to Storrington, and later to Washington, and I ignored them all. I kept my intention of resting early and often and tried to do so about every hour. The fatigue of the walk was finally catching up with me on this day: my legs were tired, and so were my feet. I remembered the meltdowns I had experienced toward the end of Day 5 on my previous journey, and I resolved to be extra vigilant about resting. Now I understood why so many other walkers were taking a rest day. But instead of taking a rest day, I had opted to extend my journey from eight days to nine days, thus eliminating the extra-long day between Steyning and Alfriston.

On my usual tradition, I attempted to make the day's theme —Time to Collaborate—into a song as I walked. Unfortunately, my creative juices seemed to have run out, as the song was suspiciously similar to the one for "See the Big Picture." I had no idea what this theme meant. Was I expected to collaborate with someone this day on the walk, or was it a theme for my life? When I had been thinking of creative projects on Day 2, they had been collaborative projects, so perhaps I had already covered this theme? Only time would tell.

It wasn't raining, but it was very windy up on the ridge. While it had started out as a pleasant breeze, after a few hours of walking, the wind was starting to get tedious. I kept trying to find more protected spots to sit for a rest, but it wasn't easy. This meant that my breaks were reasonably short, as it seemed to be easier to keep walking in the wind than it was to rest in it.

The trail started to head downhill toward the busy A24 road, which was thankfully reasonably easy to cross. The track rose fairly steeply—once again, by South Downs Way standards—to a small car park. I knew I was approaching Chanctonbury Ring, and I remembered just how hot and tired and miserable I had been at this point in the journey four years prior. Halfway up the hill, I stopped for another rest. I didn't want another meltdown at the end of this afternoon. This time, I found a little grassy spot at a turnoff for another footpath, and I took my shoes off for the first time that day. My system was still working: I had a couple of tiny blisters, but nothing that even warranted Compeed. They were easy enough to manage.

Once my feet were dry, I changed my socks and got up to continue my journey. The trail rose steeply once more, then proceeded to ascend more gently as it circled around the hillside. It was getting windier and windier as I approached the top of the hill, where Chanctonbury Ring was located. The trail was once again wide open and unprotected, so I headed straight for the trees of the Ring in the hopes that they might offer protection from the wind. Not so. I wandered around looking for a protected spot, and finding none, I returned to the main trail and continued onward, stopping a bit further on for a very brief rest. I remembered there were benches at some point, but I wasn't sure how far away they were.

There were still wide open views all around, with a clear view of the sea on my right. It seemed so close, and I wondered if that had something to do with the wind, which seemed to be at its peak: there were no trees, no high points between the Way and the coast. I started seeing signs for trails that led to Steyning, and I knew I was getting close to Bramber, my destination for that afternoon. I remembered how terrible I had felt at this point on the trail and how blistered and sore my feet had been. Not so this time! I spied the first of two benches and sat down on one for what I thought would be my last rest stop of the day (not so—there would be one more). I lingered here: I knew that I only had about an hour more to go, and I was tired. I wanted the rest of my journey to be enjoyable, rather than just a means to get to my destination as it had been my first time around. I took off my shoes and let my feet air out once more.

Finally, it was time to move on. I followed the trail past fields of pigs to my right. Some were eating, others just standing around outside their shelters. There were signs along the trail urging walkers not to feed the pigs any food scraps, to avoid foot and mouth disease. I had nothing to feed them, anyway. These were the first, and only, pigs I would cross paths with on the South Downs. I didn't remember them from my first journey in 2015, but perhaps I had been feeling too poorly to notice them? Or maybe they were new here.

Eventually, the trail led down into the village of Botolphs, which I didn't remember at all from my first journey. This was one of those locations that formed a complete blank in my memory. The byway that led to a road headed gently downhill and was protected by trees. For the first time in hours, I finally felt some relief from the wind.

After passing through Botolphs, I saw the sign for the old church just off the trail. I paused and considered visiting it, but I had been there twice before when walking the Downs Link, so I decided to continue onward to Bramber. Shortly after, I reached the point where the South Downs Way meets the Downs Link, a 37 mile (60 km) trail that links the North Downs Way with the South Downs Way and then continues three miles onward to the coast. I knew there was a bench here, as I had stopped there a few times before. The bench had since been replaced and was made of freshly cut wood.

I sat down in the shade and took off my shoes and socks. A dog walker came by and asked, "Sore feet?" I replied that they were tired feet, and she carried on. Two cyclists that I had seen earlier passed me. One of them called out that they had gotten sidetracked at the pub, though I couldn't imagine which pub they meant. The trail had been so remote that day. Perhaps in Washington? They were cycling, so it was faster and easier for them to make detours from the main trail.

Looking at my guidebook, I estimated that I had just a half-hour or so to go. I could take the Downs Link to my left, as I had on my first walk when the signage was unclear (which was no longer the case), or I could continue straight ahead down the South Downs Way to the River Adur, then turn left to follow the riverbank into Bramber and Upper Beeding. I remembered my small meltdown when I stepped off the tree-lined Downs Link and opted for the riverbank, which I followed all the way into the twin villages, turning left to enter Bramber. Not surprisingly, my hotel seemed much closer than it had four years earlier. It appeared my frequent breaks had made a difference this year.

The Evening

Upon arrival at The Castle Inn, I was quickly shown to my room, which was much tinier than the one I had previously stayed in. Still, it had what I needed—a comfortable bed, a chair, a kettle and tea making supplies, and a clean bathroom—and so I dropped my pack onto the floor and prepared for my daily routine. After showering, washing my clothes, and making my first cup of tea, I settled in to write this chapter. And then I thought about dinner. I hadn't been thrilled with dinner at The Castle Inn four years prior, and while it was indeed possible things had improved, I perused the information guide for other dinner options.

There were a few restaurants in the village, and I decided on Indian food, so I phoned up and made a reservation for dinner. When the time came, I walked the two minutes or so down the street, and entered to find a totally empty restaurant. There was plenty of staff, but no other diners, despite it being Friday night. I was shown to a table where I looked over the menu. It seemed that this would be a quiet dinner alone, unlike the previous two nights. And so it was.

I read a book on my iPad as I silently ate my dinner and then headed back to The Castle Inn for the rest of the evening. The village was charming, something I hadn't noticed the first time I had stayed there, but I was too tired to wander around much. I went straight to my room and settled in for the night.

DAY 6

P anther–Reclaim Your Power was the theme. I liked the sound of that! Personal power was something that I had always struggled with—there were many times in my life when I felt powerless. So I relished the thought of reclaiming my power.

The Morning

My alarm went off when I was in the middle of a dream, which meant that it took a while for me to fully come to my senses. Because I was staying at an inn and not a B&B, I hadn't needed to request my breakfast at a specific time, so I could be flexible with my morning routine. Still, I planned to go down at about 8:30, which seemed to be my preferred breakfast hour on this trip. In retrospect, if I had realized just how short this stage of the walk was, I would have taken advantage of this and slept in later.

The inn had several rooms and was the largest place I would be staying on the South Downs. This meant that the dining room was packed full of people when I arrived. There was a large table of maybe ten or twelve people and another table with the three couples from the east coast whom I hadn't seen at all on the trail the previous day. The Australians I had seen in the village after I had dinner, so I knew they were still more or less on track with me. Everyone else had disappeared, though I still thought I might catch up with the California sisters this day, as they had stayed the previous night further on the trail and would be staying this night in the same village as I was.

After a quick breakfast, I was ready to pack up and get going. My cold had settled into a slight cough, but I knew this would probably be my last chance for cough syrup until I reached the end of my walk, so I headed straight to the pharmacy after checking out of the hotel. I was advised on the best non-drowsy cough syrup, which I took a swig of before placing it on the side of my back before getting straight back to my walk. I returned by the same riverside trail and soon joined the South Downs Way once more.

The Walk

This part of the trail was vaguely familiar to me, as it coincided with the Downs Link for a bit before splitting once more into two paths. There was a water tap just before the road, and I filled up my water bottle with fresh, cold water. I always opted to fill my bottles on the trail when possible. Somehow, the water tasted fresher and cleaner than village water, which sometimes had too much of a chlorine taste to it. The day was a bit breezy, but nothing like the wind from the previous day. Still, I was thankful for my light fleece.

It was a Saturday morning, and there were more people out on the trail than there had been on previous days. I had passed the Australians near the water tap, and then I was passed by a group of young walkers in bright yellow high visibility vests.

The trail crossed a road and headed steadily up Truleigh Hill. I remembered this stage of the walk being dark, foggy, and drizzly on my previous journey. Today I could see the beautiful views all around: rolling fields to my left and right and the coastline far beyond to the south. There was a large offshore wind farm in the water, which I later learned was Rampion Wind Farm. Located between 8–16 miles (between 13–25 kilometers) from the shore, the wind farm is situated off the Sussex coast. It is named after the rampion flower, the official flower of Sussex.

I planned to fill up my water reservoir with fresh water at the Truleigh Hill YHA youth hostel, something I should have done at the first water tap when I filled my bottle. I had been topping up my reservoir each day, but it was tasting funny, and I thought it was past time I replaced it with fresh water from the tap. Soon enough, I arrived at the hostel. I set my pack on a picnic table, took out my reservoir, and dumped the water on the grass before reading the sign that the tap was out of service, and I'd have to head up to the kitchen on the first floor. That was out of the question. Instead, I filled it with the water from my bottle and planned to fill that later on. Thankfully, this seemed to be the day of water taps; there were several of them on this stretch of the Way.

I was passed by several young walkers, a Scouts group. There were dog walkers out, and plenty of day walkers. Even though I wasn't anywhere near the trailheads, there was a notable difference between the weekdays and weekend days on the South Downs. The trail passed through Truleigh Hill Farm, then headed down, up, and down again over rolling hills as it approached Fulking Hill. The sky was full of paragliders and hang gliders, their wings brightly colored in the sky. I paused from time to time to watch them, eventually sitting down in the grass to take my first break of the day. I went through my guidebook as I rested, trying to figure out how I had managed to plan a longer journey the previous day and a shorter one on this day. I had thought it would make for two ten-mile days, but in reality, it was more like twelve and eight. That explained why I had been so tired on the previous day. The guidebook recommended stopping in Steyning, not in Bramber or Upper Beeding, the twin villages where I had stayed. Because the book suggested taking the first turnoff to Steyning, rather than the one that was closer to Bramber, it made for two almost equal days of walking. The way I had split things up, I had come off the trail much further on, essentially taking two miles off this day's walk and adding them to the previous day. I wasn't sure how I felt about a shorter day: in reality, I felt like I needed a bit of a rest, but it felt wrong to be out on the trail for less time. I resolved to rest even more often, if I could, to stretch out the day.

At this point, I remembered to consult the day's theme: "Reclaim your power." I was reminded of The Grandmothers chapter from my recent book *If Trees Could Talk: Life Lessons from the Wisdom of the Woods*, which was all about personal power. This was something I had struggled with throughout my life, though I was certainly improving.

In that chapter, The Grandmothers had explained what personal power actually meant, and they had given readers an oath to take which would help them step into their personal power and feel more grounded in life:

"Personal power is a feeling ... and it is multi-layered. It is not something that most people will achieve overnight, or after one simple visualization. It is made up of the layers of self-trust, self-love, self-acceptance, self-esteem, self-confidence, self-value, self-worth. And it is the sense of all of these things being deeply grounded and connected with all the multiple layers of your being: your conscious mind, your subconscious mind, your superconscious

*mind. It is your regular everyday self, connected with your Higher
Self, or soul, or whatever it is that you personally choose to call it.
The more you can do to connect with all these parts of you and
to activate and amplify self-love and self-acceptance and self-trust,
all of that work, this multi-layered, multi-dimensional work, will
help contribute to your own sense of personal power."*

Getting up from my rest, I continued down the Way,
crossing a quiet lane and continuing on through grassland that
was dotted here and there with shrubs and hawthorn trees. I
was desperate for a pit stop, but there were people all around.
In addition to all the walkers, there was an orienteering group
out. I wandered off the trail into a grove of hawthorn trees,
finding a semi-private spot that seemed to do the trick. When I
was finishing, I saw a small black container hanging from the
hawthorn right in front of me; as I suspected, it was a geocache.
I didn't feel like taking the time to sign it, so I replaced it as I
had found it, pleased to have discovered a geocache that I
hadn't even been searching for. That was always a fun surprise.

Geocaching is, according to the official website: "a real-
world, outdoor adventure that is happening all the time, all
around the world. To play, participants use the Geocaching app
and/or a GPS device to navigate to cleverly hidden containers
called geocaches. There are millions of geocaches in 190 coun-
tries waiting to be discovered—there are probably even some
near you right now." I loved searching for geocaches on my
walks, and it was even more fun to come across one unex-
pectedly.

I came out onto the trail about the same time as another
lone daywalker, and we began chatting about the path as we
went. He confirmed that I was indeed very near the WildFlour
Cafe at Saddlescombe Farm and that Pyecombe would be just
an hour after that. This was disheartening as I didn't want my
day's walking to be over that soon. I stopped for another rest,

and he continued on. Though I probably didn't need it, I took my shoes and socks off. I was trying to stretch out my rest stops as much as possible.

Getting up after my break, I walked onward and headed down a small hill toward the road, which I crossed and then entered Saddlescombe Farm, a National Trust property. Saddlescombe Farm dates back to prehistoric times—though we can only imagine what it was called back then—and a variety of archaeological discoveries have been made in the area, including Bronze Age loom weights and axe heads, and Mesolithic arrowheads. It eventually changed hands from Saxons to Normans and appears in the Domesday survey of 1086, with the first detailed record of the farm. It was later managed by the Knights Templar. It is perhaps best known for its donkey wheel, a huge wooden wheel that would have been powered by a donkey or a small horse to draw water from the 164-foot (50-meter) deep well.

I decided to linger here, having tea and cake at the cafe before exploring the information barn and later filling up my water bottle at the tap. I then ventured on to see the donkey wheel, which was located down a narrow path overgrown with stinging nettles, which were impossible to avoid. The donkey wheel was worth seeing, but the nettles were unforgiving. Braving the nettles again on my way back to the trail, I returned to the South Downs Way. My legs were bright pink and stinging fiercely. However, I knew that nettles had plenty of health benefits when cooked and eaten or drunk as a tea, so I cheerfully tried to convince myself that there was undoubtedly a therapeutic effect to being stung by them.

The trail headed up a grassy hillside, with open views of rolling hills all around. I kept turning around to see the view of patchwork fields behind me. The coast was still off to my right. After I crested the top of the hill and came down the other side, I could see the twin Jack and Jill windmills on the side of another hill in the distance. I knew I was approaching Pyecombe, and it was still quite early.

I tried to make a song out of my daily theme, but I just wasn't into it. I walked down the hill, passing a man sitting under a hawthorn tree. We greeted each other, and he later caught up to me just before I reached the busy A23 road. He lived in Brighton and did a lot of walking in the South Downs. We crossed the A23 bridge together, and then I paused on the other side, letting him go on as I consulted my map to see where my B&B was located.

It was just before 2pm, which I suspected was far too early to check into my B&B. I saw a text message from the host, confirming that check-in was at 4pm and that they would be out before then. I decided to stop in and visit the village church, but there was a wedding on, so I continued onward and discovered a small bench just outside the church grounds, surrounded by leafy green trees. I sat there for a good half hour, deciding what to do for two hours. A few drops of water fell from the sky, and I headed down the street to visit the pub for a pint and a snack before checking in. It was also the perfect amount of time to write up this day's chapter.

The Evening

I kept an eye on the clock as I ate and wrote, and when I was ready, I paid my bill and headed back up the road to my B&B. The hosts had already arrived, and I was shown to my room, a comfortable twin-bedded room overlooking the garden. I set my pack down, pulled everything out that I would need to shower and change, and walked across the hallway to the shared bathroom. As I undressed and got ready to shower and then wash my clothes, I saw a small, handwritten note on the wall next to the sink: the washing of clothes was not permitted.

I stood there, open-mouthed. This was a B&B on the South

Downs Way. If I didn't wash my clothes tonight, I wouldn't have anything to wear the day after tomorrow! What was I going to do? I showered, worried about this, and went back across the hall to my room to ponder the situation. I suffer from a weird combination of being annoyed by rules that don't make sense (to me) and a fear of not following those rules. I imagine that some messy walkers must have dripped water all over the bathroom and/or bedroom at some point, which must have led to this ridiculous rule. I eventually resolved that if I left no evidence of my washing, then there would be no problem with it. By this point, I was skilled in washing my clothes in my B&B bathroom and getting them dry without making a mess, so I was confident I could do the same here. And so I did.

Dinner time came and went. I wasn't hungry after my late afternoon snack, so I opted to stay in and rest. Plus, that way, I could ensure that no one would enter my room and see my clothes drying neatly on my towels. I had a leisurely read before turning out the light to sleep. My legs were still stinging of nettles that evening as I drifted off.

DAY 7

Deer–Bring a Gentle Touch was the oracle of the day. I liked the sound of that. Would this be an easy day on the trail? Or would I come across a situation which needed to be handled gently?

The Morning

Still nervous about my clothes drying in my room, I headed down to breakfast, which was held at a shared table with another couple, who were in the area for a wedding, though not the wedding I had seen at the village church. We chatted as we ate, and then I headed back up to my room to pack everything up. My clothes hadn't dried very much overnight, and I clipped my socks to my drying system and put everything in the top of my pack before going downstairs to check out. I double-checked that I hadn't left anything damp or dripping and that there was no evidence of my washing.

The Church of the Transfiguration in Pyecombe is a Grade I Listed building that was apparently first built-in 1170. There was no wedding this morning, and so I entered the church and had a look around before walking up the road to rejoin the Way. The church is home to one of just six remaining Tapsel gates, all of which can be found within 10 miles (16 km) of Lewes. A Tapsel gate is mounted on a central pivot, unlike most gates, which are mounted on one side or the other. One of the other examples of a Tapsel gate can be found in Botolphs, near Bramber.

The Walk

From Pyecombe, the Way crossed a reasonably busy road before heading up into a golf course. It was before 9:30, but there were already golfers out on the green. The day was clear, with a deep blue sky and puffy white clouds. It felt like it was going to be a warm one. The trail climbed steadily through the golf course, passing a pretty table and benches to the left of the path. If it hadn't been so early in the day, it would have been the perfect stop for a rest. I felt fully recovered from my previous exertions: the short day's walk, combined with a good night's rest, had helped a great deal.

It was a Sunday morning, so there were a few day walkers out. Cyclists passed from time to time. It looked as though they were just out for the day, and not walking the length of the South Downs Way. I thought I might see the three couples from the east coast at some point since I had greeted them as I came out of the pub the previous afternoon, but they were nowhere in sight at any point during the day.

The Jack and Jill windmills were off in the distance, to the left of the trail. It would be just a 10-15 minute detour to visit them, but unfortunately, Jill was only open in the afternoon. The Clayton windmills stand above the village of Clayton, in West Sussex, and are Grade II Listed buildings. They have been featured in the film *The Black Windmill*, with Michael Caine. Jane dates back to 1821, and Jack was added several years later in 1866. Jill continues to be a working windmill, producing locally grown organic wheat, which is primarily sold to visitors. Jack is privately owned.

It was at about this point that I caught up with the Australian couple. We chatted for a bit about the places we had stayed in Pyecombe. They were delighted with their B&B, and I lamented about the no-washing rule, which they also considered unreasonable. Then I carried on. They had a longer day than I, as they were stopping further on down the trail in Rodmell. There were so many ways of dividing up this trail into different stages; so far, I was delighted with how I had done on this journey.

I remembered how I had felt walking this long stretch between Bramber and Lewes, and how worried I had been about whether or not I would make it. I wondered what it would have been like to complete the same long day this time around, now that the weather was so much cooler. I knew I *could* have done it; I had managed before in the hot weather. But this second South Downs experience was more about enjoying the journey than it was pushing myself to see what I could do. So far, it was turning out to be much, much more enjoyable than my previous experience.

There were exceptional views all around: patchwork fields of different shades of golden yellow and green, with the occasional glimpse of the sea off to my right. Brighton was also visible off in the distance. I tried to ignore focusing on any evidence of civilization—it seemed to represent some strange, foreign world to me as I walked this peaceful trail—and I kept my eye on the hills. I could see another offshore wind farm in the water—or maybe it was the same one? I later learned that it was.

I came out on the other side of the golf course, and the trail turned left and then sharply right near some stables. Horses were pastured in fields off to the left of the trail. Once more, the

path, which was a wide and comfortable track, rose steadily up
the hillside as it approached Ditchling Beacon. I had walked
this portion of the trail a few times before, not just on my
previous South Downs Way experience but as a portion of a
route from Hassocks to Lewes. The path crossed through a
grassy field where sheep grazed. There were spiny gorse bushes
off to the left of the trail. The occasional cyclists passed me by,
as did several runners.

The trail started to head gently downhill toward the car
park, where I had stopped for ice cream on my previous journey. Alas, it was not even eleven in the morning, and the ice
cream van had not yet arrived. I was still full from breakfast,
but that didn't stop me from feeling just a bit disappointed. It
was a Sunday morning, and the car park was packed; this probably was where many of the walkers, runners, and cyclists I had
seen had started their journey.

I crossed a quiet road and headed gently uphill and then
downhill. To the left were views of the High Weald and
Ashdown Forest off in the distance. The Weald is the area
between the North and South Downs and is made of up three
separate parts: the High Weald, which is what I could see from
where I was, the Low Weald, and the Greensand Ridge, which
was located near where I lived. The name Weald means woodland in Old English, and this region was once covered in forest.
The trees had long since been felled to create the rolling hills of
farmland that can be seen today.

To the right, Brighton was still visible off in the distance,
but I continued to pretend it did not exist. The trail was wide
open, with no shade, though the level track made for easy walking. I saw paths off to the left leading down to Plumpton, where
I knew there was a good pub for lunch. But it was still early in
the day, and I didn't plan on eating until dinner, so I carried on.

Before I knew it, I reached the point where the trail
continued three miles ahead to Lewes, as I had done four years

prior, or turned to the right to stay on the South Downs Way. It seemed quite early in the day; perhaps I could have combined these two days into one long walk as I had four years earlier. Still, it had been good to have a shorter day to rest up a bit, since I didn't plan a full rest day like others had. I turned right, curious as to what this stretch of the path looked like since I had missed it the last time I had walked the trail.

Here, the South Downs Way was a very narrow path that cut straight between fields, with a wire fence to the left that was bordered with the occasional hawthorn tree. I had to jump to the side several times as cyclists came past. Some of them were so silent that I didn't hear them until they were just behind me. I was so focused on the trail ahead that it was as though the trail behind—and anyone who may be coming up behind me —ceased to exist.

The path turned to the right, continuing alongside a hedge. Then it turned to the left and climbed sharply through a little woodland of hollies and beeches. I slowed down, taking my time as I ascended the slope. I knew I was already more than halfway to my destination that day, and I was in no rush to arrive early. Three men who were walking together came up from behind and passed me, greeting me as they did so. Soon enough, the trail exited the little wood and came out onto an open field. The men had stopped for a lunch break, waiting for their wives to catch up with them. They were doing the South Downs Way as a group, in little stages spread out over the year. We chatted a bit before I continued on.

Having gained some height on the trail, it now descended toward the A27 road. I could see tents set up in the field at Housedean Farm, and I remembered that they offered a camp-ground. When I reached the road, I consulted my map. I knew there was a service station to my left, as well as a snack van. But I wasn't hungry, and I didn't need a snack, so I turned right and followed the pavement alongside the road before turning sharp left to cross the bridge that carried the Way over the A27.

On the other side, the trail turned sharply left once more. This was very near the point where I had picked up the Way after taking the bus back from Lewes. The portion of the trail that I had skipped was lovely, but the three miles from where I had departed the South Downs Way to get into Lewes had also been pleasant, so it was really too bad that I had mentally beat myself up over missing that bit of the trail. It hadn't been a shortcut at all; it had merely been three miles in the other direction.

The path was narrow and shady, bordered on the right by bramble and hawthorns. I could see the snack van off in the distance alongside the road; it was closed, so thankfully, I hadn't sought it out for a bite to eat. Further on, I saw the service station. It would have been quite the detour, worth it if I had actually *needed* something, but a waste of time to walk alongside a busy, noisy road just to stop in and buy a cold drink. I had made the right decision.

From there, the trail turned right, went under the railway, and then turned left again. The noise from the A27 was still behind me, but I could no longer see it. I was back in Nature. The path turned right (lots of sharp turns on the Way today, as you may have noticed!) and headed up a little wooded hill, somewhat steeply. It went through a gate and came out into open fields on the other side. I stopped alongside the trail for a break, sitting in a grassy bit and taking off my shoes and socks. Several cyclists went by as I rested, as well as one woman walker who appeared to be doing the Way in the opposite direction. She asked me how far I was going that day, and then continued onward.

Getting up and hoisting my pack onto my back, I continued on. Two young men passed me in the other direction, and one of them asked me if I had seen a pub anywhere. I had not. "First world problems," he laughed, and they walked on. From there, the path climbed steadily up a golden hillside. Cows and sheep were pastured off to my left. I kept pausing as I climbed to look at the hill I had come down on the other side of the A27 not long earlier. The views all around were lovely: rolling hills in different shades of gold and green. As I reached the top of the slope, the Way turned left and followed a wire fence. At one point, another trail split off and appeared to run parallel to the one I was on. I consulted my OS Maps app, and it looked like the other track was the official Way. If I had bothered to consult my guidebook, I would have seen that it recommended following the path nearest the fence. In any case, they both came together at the corner of the field, so it made no difference.

I was nearing the end of my day, and there were two trails down into Kingston-near-Lewes: Juggs Road, a byway, and another path. I consulted the OS Maps app, and the contour lines showed a similar, equally steep descent on both trails. I planned to take the first turnoff, Juggs Lane, but somehow missed it: I didn't realize just how close I was to Kingston. To take Juggs Lane, I would have needed to go straight through a field of cows just after passing through a gate. Instead, I continued to the right.

Several minutes later, I saw a sign indicating the turnoff to Kingston, just 3/4 mile away. I consulted my map, realized what I had done, and headed downhill. It was a wide, white, chalky trail that descended steadily toward the village. On a warm, dry afternoon such as this, it was easy going, but it was supposed to rain the following morning, and I knew that would make the journey uphill a bit tricky on the slippery chalk slope. Still, one day of rain out of nine was not worth complaining about. So far, the weather had been absolutely perfect every day. I resolved to make early September my official time for walking: school was back in session, which meant that families were otherwise occupied and the trails were quiet. The summer was cooling down for autumn, and the weather was still warm, yet not hot.

I came out into the village and turned right down a footpath that seemed to border the edge of the residential neighborhood. My B&B was located two streets over, and it was easy enough to find. A couple and their small child were harvesting apples from their tree alongside the road. They had a big box full of fruit, and there were plenty of apples still on the tree. The child said to me, "We have lots of apples!" I agreed with him, laughed, and carried on toward my B&B, heading up a long drive past pretty flowering gardens to the main house.

The Evening

My hostess was there when I arrived, and she showed me into the sitting room where she served me tea and cake and then disappeared to put the finishing touches on my room. It was ready soon enough, and I set my pack down in my spacious room before filling the bathtub and settling in. After a leisurely bath, I went about with my usual routine of washing my clothes, having another cup of tea in my room, and then heading out to the local pub for dinner. It was Sunday, and so there was roast.

The Juggs is housed in a 14th-century cottage with original oak beams and a log fire. The building itself is delightfully quirky and cozy, and the Sunday roast was spectacular. By the time I arrived, they only had three plates of pork belly left, a dish that I'm really not a fan of, but it was fantastic. Both the pub and Juggs Lane (which you may remember from earlier) are named after the baskets that were used by Brighton fishwives who passed through Kingston-near-Lewes on their way to the Lewes market.

I took my time eating my dinner at my tiny little table in the corner and writing up this chapter after I finished my meal. I then headed back to Nightingales, where the B&B cat Claude meowed outside my door not long after I installed myself in my room. I opened it and let him in until he tired of the visit and returned to the sitting room.

I reflected on the day's theme as I went to bed: Bring a Gentle Touch. All in all, it had been a gentle day's walk. It had been smooth going, and everything had been quite easy.

DAY 8

M oth–Surrender Now was the daily oracle. What would I need to surrender to? Would I have intrusive thoughts or worries plaguing my mind on this day's walk? Would I need to surrender to the reality of a rainy day on the trail? I often found it difficult to let go of control and surrender to my circumstances, so I suspected this might be a challenging day.

The Morning

After the best night's sleep I had had all week—the combination of an early night to bed on an excellent mattress made for nine-plus hours of sleep—and a lovely cooked breakfast, I was ready to brave the long uphill hike to get back on the South Downs Way. It had rained already—either during the night or early that morning—and intermittent rain was predicted all afternoon. I was not looking forward to this, but it would be a small price to pay for the perfect weather I had had every other day.

With just two more days of walking to go, I was nearing the

end of my journey, and I wasn't happy about it. This South Downs experience had been absolutely perfect in every way: weather, blisters, and general happiness. This had been a truly joyful week, and I wasn't looking forward to it ending. In fact, if I had had the time to turn around in Eastbourne and walk the whole thing again in the other direction, I would have done so. But I was entering a busy time of the year, and my calendar was booked. I was, however, looking forward to machine-washed clothes that felt fresh and clean, rather than my sink-washed ones that never felt 100% fresh.

The Walk

I departed Nightingales B&B and found my way back to the path that led up to the South Downs Way. Though it had rained, the chalk track was not at all slippery, and it was easy going. I slowly and steadily climbed the hill, pausing to look at a giant black slug oozing its way across the path. I decided to see it as a reminder to take things slowly on this day: not only did I not want my walk to end, but I had an extra couple of miles to walk today, and I wanted to rest and keep my feet feeling fresh.

I soon reached the top of the hill and rejoined the South Downs Way. The sky was ominous and overcast, covered with dark gray clouds, but it wasn't raining. Off in the distance, the sky above Lewes was even darker, and it looked like it was furiously pouring rain there. I was thankful that I had at least been able to ascend the steep chalky track without rain. Now that I was once more at the top of the ridge, the Way was relatively flat and smooth going. It was windy and a bit chilly. I had left the B&B wearing trousers rather than shorts, and I had my fleece on as well. It looked like I was in for another windy day, perhaps with rain on top of it.

The trail became a paved track that cut through two fields.

The left-hand field was bordered with about two meters of wheat, which hadn't been harvested, and the right-hand field was bordered with the same width of wildflowers. The diversity of the flowers was surprising: there were every color and type of local wildflower, which made me wonder if they had been planted with the idea of helping local wildlife or bees or... something. Perhaps it was to aid bees with pollination for the fields? I had no idea, but it was pleasantly unusual.

I enjoyed the extensive views all around: farmland to my left, with Lewes off in the distance (still being rained on) and a city to my right, on the coast. Could it be Brighton, still? I wasn't sure. I could see another offshore wind farm—or perhaps it was the eastern bit of the same one I had seen on previous days —in the water.

After crossing a little lane, the track became grassy once more. It also started to look familiar, and I remembered a particular sign from my last South Downs journey. Soon enough, I came across it: the Greenwich meridian fingerpost sign, with one finger pointing to the western hemisphere and the other pointing to the eastern hemisphere. It seemed so strange to come across the sign in the middle of a field, but this portion of the South Downs Way coincided with the Greenwich Meridian Trail.

Not long after, the Way narrowed down and began to follow a chain-link fence on my right, which turned into a wooden privacy fence. I started to see signs warning of traffic ahead, and I came out onto a lane in between two houses. I crossed it and went through a gate into a field, where I sat down on a memorial bench. The little lane indicated that Rodmell was not far away, and I wondered if I would pass the Australians at some point.

After a brief rest, I got up and continued down the path, which dropped very steeply down near a farm. A small cornfield bordered the trail off to my right, and in the field next to it sat massive, round bales of hay. When I reached the bottom, the Way turned right down a farm track that cut between fields full of round bales. It had been a peaceful Monday morning on the trail, and I hadn't yet crossed paths with anyone: there were no walkers, runners, or cyclists out. I was back to the peace and quiet of a weekday on the South Downs.

The path turned right, heading uphill to a road. I could hear a train off in the distance, and I knew I was approaching Southease. When I reached the road, I was unclear which way to go, but I soon realized I needed to turn right to head down into the tiny village of Southease. I went straight to the church, where I knew I could fill up my water reservoir, which was getting low. But first, I entered the church to have a look around. The Church of St Peter in Southease has a nave that dates back to the 11th Century and is possibly pre-Conquest. That and the round tower dating to the mid-12th Century remain, and it is home to wall paintings dating to the 13th Century. I neglected to visit the church on my first South Downs walk, and I really enjoyed my visit this time around. It's well worth a peek inside.

Coming out of the church, I sat down on one of the benches to rest. It was absolutely quiet in the village; no one was out. After a few minutes, I added water to my reservoir and continued my journey. I knew I'd be stopping very soon at the youth hostel for a more extended break. I followed the little lane out of the village and crossed the River Ouse on a wooden bridge. I wanted to pause and take a picture, but it was so windy I feared my phone would be whipped from my hands, so I kept going.

Shortly after, I came upon Southease Station, a bizarre little railway station in the middle of nowhere. The village of Southease can't have much more than ten houses in it, and Lewes isn't that far away. It's a miracle that the station is still open, with hourly trains in each direction. There are two ways of getting across the tracks on foot: a footbridge heading up and over the railway, or a level crossing. A green light indicated that it was safe to cross, so I opted for the level crossing and hurried across the tracks.

Just up ahead was the youth hostel, and I decided to go in for a cup of tea. To my surprise, I found Richard in the courtyard. He was back from his rest day near Amberley and was continuing on his journey, stopping the night in Alfriston as everyone else seemed to be doing. He had been at the hostel for a while and had seen the Australians an hour before. It looked like I wouldn't be crossing paths with them this day.

Richard soon continued on his journey, and I went in for tea...and cake. It wasn't quite noon, and I'd had a filling breakfast, but cake seemed appropriate for some reason. I carried my tray out to the patio where I could take my shoes off as I ate. There was no one else in the cafe.

My rest was over soon enough, and I headed back on the trail, crossing the busy A26 via a pretty wooden bridge. I could see people on top of the hill I would soon be climbing, but their silhouettes were bizarre. It looked like they were carrying umbrellas—but that couldn't be. It wasn't raining, and it was far too windy for an umbrella. Were they actually people, or were they scarecrows, planted to ward off birds from some crop at the top of the hill? At that point, I had no idea.

The trail wound around the hillside, then headed more steeply up it. A lone runner passed me, going in the opposite direction. He didn't look like he was carrying anything strange. Off in the distance, further up the hill and to the left of the trail, I saw another peculiar silhouette moving up the hill. What was going on? As I crested the hill, I saw four men off to the left of the path. It looked like they all had model airplanes with them, which explained the strange silhouettes: they must have carried them up the hillside by holding them over their heads. Mystery solved, I greeted them and continued onward.

The path continued through open fields and pastures. There were views down to Newhaven and Seaford to my right, off in the distance on the coast. The trail rose a bit and continued along the top of the ridge. It was still tranquil on the path. I saw a small car park off in the distance, with a horse trailer and a couple of horses. I sat down for a short rest but felt a handful of raindrops on me, so I quickly got up to continue my journey. I had thought I might be able to out-walk the rain if it followed me from Lewes, and it seemed that I managed to do so.

The trail went through a gate and continued through grassy fields, parallel to the gate. A lone cyclist had passed me, but then returned and came through the gate, lamenting that he had missed the turnoff. It was still windy—but not rainy—and from the looks of it, there was always wind on this hilltop. The poor hawthorns were all windblown toward the east and looked like they were pointing South Downs walkers in the direction of Alfriston, and later Eastbourne.

I passed a trig point on my left, and what looked like a sunken tumulus, probably damaged by excavation. A trig point, or triangulation station, is a small concrete pyramid that was used for surveying in the days before GPS. You can still find them on hilltops around the world.

To my right, on the other side of the fence, was a small long barrow. There had been a lot of tumuli along the South Downs Way, which indicated that this trail cut through many ancient settlements. Or perhaps the settlements had been down in the valleys below, and only the dead were buried up high on the ridges.

The Way descended down to the little car park near the Bo-Peep farmhouse, and I saw a man off to the left of the trail, throwing a ball to his dog, which paused as it watched me walk by. The track rose just after the car park, ascending Bostal Hill. As it got higher, I could see Arlington Reservoir off in the distance to the left of the trail, down in the valley. To the right, I could still see Seaford.

On the other side of Bostal Hill, the trail made its last descent into Alfriston. As I went through a gate, I saw an information board off to the right of the path, and I went to investigate. Long Burgh long barrow is an unchambered burial mound that probably dates back to the Early Neolithic period, and is one of just ten recorded long barrows in Sussex. It has not been restored in any way, and it was quite a surprise to me. I didn't remember it from my first journey down the Way.

From there, the trail became a narrow, white chalky path alternating with paved sections that descended between hedges of hawthorn and bramble, with the occasional sloe-covered blackthorn. It came out into the more modern residential part of Alfriston before dropping down onto the main road, with my accommodation for the night, The George Inn, sitting straight in front of me. Despite the sky looking ominous all day, it didn't rain once. It had been yet another dry day on the trail. I checked in at the bar to find that not only was I the only guest for the night but that I had been given an upgrade to their suite. It was a delightful surprise, and I was so grateful to have a bathtub on my final night on the South Downs Way.

The Evening

Alfriston is a pretty little village that sits just off the Downs in the Cuckmere River Valley. In fact, it's so pretty that it's really the highlight of the week. The High Street is home to the village's three historic pubs, one of which—The Star Inn—dates back to 1345. If you arrive early enough in the day, it's worth quickly showering so you can enjoy a walk around the village—which is precisely what I did when I arrived.

The first time I walked the South Downs Way, I had forgotten to bring my National Trust card, and so I missed out on a visit to the 14th Century Alfriston Clergy House, which was the very first property bought by the National Trust, in 1896. This time, I was determined to see the building, even though there wasn't much time left to explore when I arrived. The little timber-framed thatched cottage is absolutely lovely, and it's been furnished as it may have been back when it was first built. Both the house and the gardens are well worth a visit.

I toured the clergy house until it closed, and then I wandered around the village a bit before heading back to The George Inn for one of the most lovely dinners I had had all week. It was a weekday evening, and the pub was relatively quiet, so I lingered with a book before going up to my room to rest. It was my last night on the trail, and I was already starting to miss the South Downs Way, despite having one final day of walking ahead of me.

And what of the day's oracle, Surrender Now? I suppose I had surrendered to the flow of the day on the trail. I certainly hadn't come up against anything challenging.

DAY 9

L izard–Dream the World into Being was the oracle for my last day on the South Downs Way. It sounded delightful: the perfect theme for this day, which would be a transition from trail life to everyday life. It was a reminder that I could create my own reality based on my dreams.

The Morning

After what felt like hours, I finally managed to get a good night's sleep. I had that same excited anticipation I had experienced the night before starting out. This week on the South Downs had been such a lovely experience, and I wasn't ready for it to end. I still had the feeling that the South Downs Way existed outside of the dimension in which my everyday life existed, and I wasn't ready to return. This was an extraordinary world I'd been living in for the past week.

I read a lot about post-trail depression from people who have walked much longer trails: the Pacific Crest Trail, the Appalachian Trail, the Camino de Santiago. But little is written about post-trail depression after a much shorter walk, like a one-week National Trail. I wouldn't say that I've ever experienced depression after a long walk, but there is undoubtedly a period of re-integration back into my normal life. The transition between finishing the trail and arriving home can feel quite abrupt, and it's much more awkward and uncomfortable than the return from a typical holiday.

I had a quiet breakfast alone at The George Inn since I was the only guest staying there (one of the benefits of passing through Alfriston on a weekday outside of the high season). After getting my pack together in my room, I checked out and headed out the back door, through the pub garden and down a little trail that led straight to the South Downs Way. There, I saw the sign that indicated the split in the path: one was the public footpath which would run mostly along the coast; the other was the public bridleway heading inland via the Long Man of Jevington. I already knew which one I was taking, so I headed down the riverside path, which was already filled with walkers.

The Walk

It was just after 9:30 on a Tuesday morning, and I was surprised to see so many people out walking. It shouldn't have been too surprising, though, as the weather was gorgeous: clear blue sky, warm but not hot. It was the standard weather I had experienced all week, with one exception: as I walked, I could see that while some of the walkers looked like day walkers, others looked like they might be doing the South Downs Way. An older couple passed me with larger backpacks. I hadn't seen them before, but they didn't look like day walkers.

The trail closely followed the Cuckmere River. I remembered the fields being full of cows the last time I had been through here, but there were none this morning. I caught up with the three couples from the east coast and chatted with one of them for a few minutes. Then they all paused, and I continued on. The trail soon turned away from the river to come out into the tiny village of Litlington, which was quiet. Not a person in sight. I walked past the pub, went through a gate, and caught up with the couple who had previously passed me. They were applying sun cream, getting ready for what would clearly be a very sunny day.

The trail went straight uphill through a little field. A sign to the left of the path urged walkers to not touch, feed, or engage with the horses and ponies in any way. An electric fence had been put up, more to keep the walkers from the horses than the other way around, it seemed. From the looks of it, the landowners had had trouble with walkers getting too friendly with their animals. I unhooked the gate and entered the fenced-in footpath, then let the couple through before I hooked it back up again. They moved at a faster pace than I and were soon off in the distance.

From there, the Way went alongside pretty fields, the Litlington White Horse visible on a hillside off to the right. This horse is one of two well-known chalk figures in the area, the other being the Long Man of Wilmington, which can be seen on the other branch of the South Downs Way. It was first cut into the hillside in 1836 by four men, and it was restored in 1924 by the grandson of one of those men. Most recently, in 2016, six tons of chalk were spread over the horse to re-whiten it.

A tractor approached me, slowing as he reached a gate, where he stopped and got out to open it. I hurried through the gate, rather than going over the stile. The Way dropped steadily down through a field, with a hedge to one side. At the end of the field, woodland steps carried the trail up into the shade of Friston Forest. It was a beautiful little trail, and it was already starting to feel very un-South-Downs-like. There were a couple of dog walkers out, but no South Downs Way walkers. The east coast couples seemed to be far behind me.

Soon the trail came out into the pretty little village of West Dean. I paused at the duck pond, which had a collection of benches scattered around its edge, but I really didn't feel like I needed to rest just yet, so I continued onward, up a long stretch of steep woodland stairs up a hill and through a little forest. On the other side, I came out onto the gorgeous view of the spectacular Cuckmere Haven: a pretty, natural estuary with the Cuckmere River winding its way through the valley. At the end, the sea was just visible. This morning's walk had shown a dramatic change in scenery: riverside to woodlands to the seaside.

At Cuckmere Haven, the river loops back and forth, forming several oxbow lakes. This is a very, very popular tourist area on the weekends, for obvious reasons: it's absolutely gorgeous, and there are plenty of walking trails.

I headed straight down the hill toward the Seven Sisters Country Park Visitors Centre at Exceat, where I filled up my water bottle. I had been filling up at water taps on the trail rather than at my B&Bs whenever possible, as the trail water had less of a chlorinated taste to it. There was a big car park here, making the area easily accessible for day walkers, but there weren't too many people out. I followed the South Downs Way footpath signs up and over a hill where sheep were pastured.

Coming down the other side, I saw a bench (they were in abundance on this day; it looked as though they had saved up all the benches that could have been spread throughout the hundred miles of the Way and planted them on this segment of the trail) and I sat down for a quick rest. I was determined to retain my protocol of resting early and often, and I was eager to stretch out the day's walk as much as I could. I was in no hurry to finish my journey.

The trail continued onward, climbing steadily toward the cliffs, and I mistakenly assumed this was the first of the Seven Sisters. Later I realized that it was not. I was determined to keep track of the sisters, as I had lost count the first time I had walked the Way, but this time I lost track from the very start. As I reached the coastal cliffs, there was an abundance of signs that both implored walkers to be mindful of the cliff edge and also informed them of what to do if someone went over the side (dial 999 and ask for the Coast Guard, in case you were wondering).

I remembered just how difficult this day had been on my first South Downs adventure, but I was still feeling pretty good. Yes, my feet were tired, but they weren't aching . . . yet. There were now plenty more people out, walking the Seven Sisters, and all of them looked like day walkers. I slowly and steadily made my way up and down over the first four sisters—or five, as I thought at the time—until I got to a bench at the top of Brass Point. I consulted both my guidebook and also an information board, both of which confirmed that I was on the fourth, not the fifth, sister. It was then that I understood where my counting had gone wrong. I was just over halfway through the sisters, and I was still in no rush to finish.

A woman out walking with her dog paused to read the information board, and we struck up a conversation. She was wearing a badge for the Walk 1,000 Miles 2019 challenge, so I asked her how she was doing. She had already walked over 1,400 miles thus far. She had done the South Downs Way in its entirety in the previous year and was now working through the North Downs Way, in segments. We noticed that we both used Pacerpoles and shared a moment of delight for just how good they were. Pacerpoles always seemed to be a good conversation starter among walkers.

She continued her journey, and I got up to do the same. There were three sisters left (plus a small baby-sister) before reaching the National Trust property at Birling Gap, where I planned to have another little rest and perhaps get something to eat. It was up and down another four times before I reached Birling Gap, which was crawling with tourists. The car park was full and a large tour bus that had just arrived.

I waited in line to use the toilets, then I went into the gift shop and then the cafe before coming out and deciding to rest at one of the picnic tables. I took off my shoes and socks and waited for my feet to cool off. The number of people was overwhelming, and as soon as my feet were ready, I put my shoes and socks back on and headed back to the trail. I knew there was a snack bar just 15-20 minutes away at the Belle Tout Lighthouse B&B, and I planned to rest again there, to stretch out my day.

The Seven Sisters were now behind me, but I wasn't finished with hills. The rolling cliffs continued toward Belle Tout, which appeared to be closed. All gates leading to the property had signs saying that access was only for residents of the B&B. I climbed up and around on the trail, and I saw picnic tables and ice cream signs, but it did look very much closed. I continued onward, climbing up and down the rolling cliffs until I began the steady ascent to Beachy Head, the highest point on this day's walk.

It was a long climb. A man passed me, running up the hill. He soon stopped, turned around, and complained that the hill went on forever. He was right: it looked as though the hilltop was just up ahead, but then it went on and on. Eventually, I reached the top. There were exceptional views all around: rolling hills to the left, and calm blue sea to the right. The water was so still that it looked like a giant lake.

I approached the memorial with benches and sat down, taking off my shoes and socks. I estimated that I had less than an hour to go, and there wasn't much I could do to drag out my walk, except sit and rest. I waited until my feet were ready, then put my socks and shoes back on and continued my journey. Here, the Way was much better sign-marked than on my first trip, and I was quickly able to find the turnoff to the small chalky footpath that wound its way around the hillside. It was cool and shady, lined by brambles and shrubs. Most importantly: there were no people. I was all alone on this little trail.

Eventually, it came out on the top of the hill, joining a wide, grassy path that was bordered by pink-flowering rosebay willowherb. I could tell that I was on my final descent into Eastbourne. Before I knew it, I had reached a little information board that explained all about the South Downs Way. I asked a random man to take a picture of me, and we talked for a bit about the trail. Further down, at the base of the hill next to the kiosk, there was a new and larger sign, where he took another photo of me.

I was here. I had arrived. I dropped my pack on a chair at the kiosk and ordered a sandwich and a cold drink. I settled in to write this chapter as I waited to be picked up. I wondered if I would see any of my trail buddies as I waited. I had been so disappointed to miss Maggie and Martin at the end of my previous walk.

This time, however, I was not let down: Richard showed up, and we chatted until the kiosk closed. I took a photo of him by the South Downs Way sign, and then he went on his way. I sat on a grassy bit to the side of the trail to wait for my ride. As I was sitting close by the large sign marking the eastern end of the South Downs Way, I was able to see everyone coming off the trail. Two men I had never seen before arrived, and I took photos of them with the sign. They had done it in six days, which sounded exhausting. Before long, the east coast couples came by, and I took photos of them with the sign. I was so pleased to see them at the end of their journey. The only people who were missing were the Australians. I never saw them again.

It had been an excellent end to the South Downs Way; indeed: it felt like the adventure had come to a natural and very satisfying completion. I was so pleased to have walked the entire trail for a second time, and to have had such a different experience. Both journeys were lovely, but this one was so much easier than the first. And yet it had felt every much an adventure as it had the first time around.

I couldn't wait for my next walk, wherever that might be. I reflected on the day's theme: Dream the World into Being. I was ready to dream of all my future long-distance walks, and I couldn't wait to get started.

EPILOGUE

I n the days that followed my return from the South Downs Way, I was still in awe of how different my two experiences were. I actually felt embarrassed to have released the first edition of this book, full of such pain and discomfort. I was so excited to work on this second edition, so I could share my very different second experience. I've learned a lot since my first South Downs adventure in 2015, and from all my subsequent walks.

I'm eager to put my knowledge and experience to work on new walks for 2020 and beyond. I've been wanting to walk the Camino de Santiago (the most popular Camino Francés) for ages, but I just haven't been able to block out five weeks in my year to do it. So I've decided to approach the Camino differently: in 2020, I planned to walk the Camino Portugués and the Camino Inglés and to write books about my experiences. I have read that there are over 50 different routes to Santiago, with the five most commonly transited ones being (in order of popularity, according to the Oficina de Acogida al Peregrino or Pilgrim's Office):

- 56.8%: Camino Francés, 497 miles - 800 km
- 25%: Camino Portugués, 161/173 miles - 260/280 km
- 5.8%: Camino del Norte, 512 miles - 825 km
- 4.6%: Camino Primitivo, 199 miles - 321 km
- 4.3%: Camino Inglés, 68 miles - 110 km

Many people dream of doing a walk like the Camino Francés but, like me, can't yet fit a five-week walk into their calendar. So I want to walk two of the shorter and lesser-known Caminos and share my story with other potential pilgrims. The Camino Portugués will be the longest walk I've done yet, and I'm really looking forward to a new walking challenge. I originally planned to walk it in March 2020, well outside the hot summer months, but my plans were disrupted by COVID-19.

Spain went into lockdown much before the UK did, and so I threw my tent and camping gear into the car and took off to the woods for an extended camping trip. I ended up walking 150 miles in the two weeks that I was away, and I had an absolutely incredible time in the outdoors. It set me up with the perfect mindset to go into weeks of lockdown.

Lessons Learned

There are really only three big lessons that I learned from my previous walks and that I successfully applied in this second South Downs adventure:

1. Rest early and often. There's no rush! Walk at a leisurely pace and take rest breaks.
2. Take off shoes and socks. Air your feet out on every single break and switch between two pairs of socks throughout the day to keep feet fresh and reduce blisters.

3. Avoid the summer. Don't plan your walk in the hot summer months: even though England has a bad reputation for summer weather, it's still hotter than you want to be walking in.

PART IV

THE PLAN

WHAT TO EXPECT

The previous chapters of this book should have given you an idea of what the South Downs Way experience is like, and the following chapters will provide you with more details of the technical bits you'll need for preparing a walk.

To give you a quick idea of what the South Downs Way experience is like, you can expect the following:

- A sloping trail that winds through woodland and farmland for 100 miles, heading steeply uphill in the mornings to the ridge of the South Downs, and downhill in the evenings as you approach your accommodation for the night.
- A wealth of ancient historical sites, from Bronze Age barrows to a surprisingly well preserved Roman villa located not too far off the trail.
- Excellent signage (except for the first stage out of Winchester). It's always a good idea to bring a guidebook with maps, though you could probably get by without one (assuming you know how the

trail heads out of Winchester—if you only bring one map, it should be that one!).

- The very occasional crossing of busy A-roads, both on foot and via bridge or tunnel.
- Not much water, except for the spectacular sea views as you near the end of the journey. No lakes, no rivers to ford. There is, of course, the River Ouse near Southease and the River Arun as you approach Arundel.
- Mostly natural trails, with very little tarmac to walk on.
- Seemingly endless hours of glorious nature, often giving you the feeling of being completely enveloped by never-ending woods and fields, with the only sign of civilization being farms or tiny villages off in the distance.
- Accommodations ranging from tiny inns, B&Bs, and the occasional youth hostel. Camping is not an option for most of the route.

Staying Connected

Depending on your intentions for your trip, you may or may not care about mobile service and internet along the Way. In the first edition of this book, I included a day-by-day description of what connectivity was like during my 2015 walk. On my 2019 walk, I had no problems whatsoever with a mobile connection, and every place I stayed at had wifi.

Safety

Everyone I've spoken with since I returned from the South Downs Way seems impressed that I walked 100 miles on my own. At the time I was doing it, it felt only natural to walk alone, and in retrospect, I wouldn't have done it any other way. I relish the quiet meditative aspect that comes with solo walking in nature.

I do a lot of solo walking in England, and I always feel safe. There was no time on the South Downs Way when I felt unsafe or in danger, even during the long stretches where I was utterly alone, with no other walkers or cyclists crossing my path. I never questioned whether it was safe to be a woman alone walking the Way.

However, if you choose to walk alone, you need to be aware that you must be totally self-reliant: be vigilant about the weather, the temperature, and your water supply, especially when walking in the warmer months of the year. You must be sure that you set out each morning with more than enough water to drink, and food to keep you going until you arrive at your evening destination. I cannot stress this enough, having walked during one of the hottest weeks of the year.

I know this sounds ridiculous, but do not underestimate how hot it can be in England when you're walking alone out in the sun: carry more than enough water, and cover your head. That's all the safety you need to be concerned about. Obviously, follow your own common sense, and stay aware of your surroundings. If something doesn't feel right, pay attention to that. Only you are responsible for your own personal safety.

If you're still not convinced, Catherine Redfern of London Hiker has a blog post detailing <u>Why you CAN (and should) go hiking on your own</u>. Check it out.

PREPARING FOR YOUR WALK

There are some questions you might want to ask yourself before you decide to walk the South Downs Way. Are you sure this trail is right for you? Maybe you'd prefer a different National Trail or national park, or somewhere else entirely. Do the South Downs have what you want in terms of local history, scenery, and accommodations?

What are your reasons for walking the Way? What do you want to get out of it? Is this for fun, to go on a solo retreat, or are you looking to get some exercise outdoors? Or is it something else?

Who do you want to walk with? Are you planning a solo walking holiday, as I did, or would you prefer to go with a partner or with friends? I came across one other single woman, a solo man, and a few couples during my first walk. The second time around, I saw a couple of small groups, a few couples, and a couple of solo walkers.

When do you want to walk the Way? If your walk falls during BST, then you'll have long days. But summers can be hot. Perhaps consider late spring after summer time starts, or early autumn before the time changes again. Personally, I found the weather in early September to be ideal.

How are you going to walk the Way? Are you a daywalker at heart, a weekend walker, or a through walker? Some people walk the Way all in one go, as I did. Some people do West Hemisphere and East Hemisphere separately (the Way crosses through the Meridian Line). Some people walk it in two-day stages over a series of weekends. Do what works for you.

Finally, are you sure you want to walk the South Downs, rather than cycle or ride it? This is one of just two National Trails that you can also cycle or ride on horseback from point to point. There's more than one way to make the journey from Winchester to Eastbourne.

Plan Well

Asking yourself the above questions and getting clear on your answers can help you to plan well. You'll need to plan your trip before you book accommodation, before you pack, and before you start out each day. When you're out on a long-distance walk, you can't plan enough—especially if you're walking alone.

Things to consider when booking accommodation: how far off the trail your lodging is and how you want to spend the night (B&B, inn, hostel, camping). If your accommodation is more than a mile off the Way, plan to walk on the trail to the closest point to that village and get transport if you can (a good guidebook will give you an idea of whether this is possible). Or simply walk the extra distance, and plan to have a more extended day of walking.

Make sure your lodging is as close as possible to the Way. Select a place in a village close to the trail, preferably one that is the closest to the path. Avoid extra walking if you can, especially if you'll be doing the trail during the hot summer days. At the end of a long day, there's no need to add an extra two or three miles onto the walk just to reach your B&B...unless you want an extra challenge.

For example, in Lewes, I walked an extra mile that day because my B&B was on the farther end of the town...and an additional three miles because Lewes was so far from the South Downs. The second time I walked the South Downs Way, I stayed much closer to the trail: in Kingston-near-Lewes, rather than in Lewes itself. In Bramber, it would have been better to stay in Upper Beeding, which was equidistant from the trail, and it was closer to shop where I got my sandwich (and other amenities). However, I stayed at the same inn in 2019, and the walk from the trail to my accommodation was perfectly fine. In Alfriston, my B&B was located a ten-minute walk outside the main village, which meant an additional walk into dinner and back onto the trail the following day—in 2019, I stayed right in the central part of the village, which was perfect.

Plan your packing list well, and carefully evaluate everything before you put your pack together. Once you're ready, weigh your pack (including two to three quarts/liters of water and any snacks you plan to bring) and then re-evaluate the contents of your backpack. My pack felt comfortable...until I added all that water. Remember: if you're traveling outside of the hot summer months, you won't need to start out each morning with as much water on your back.

Also, plan ahead to determine whether you'll want to carry your water in bottles or in a bladder/reservoir. I ended up getting a reservoir for my Downs Link walk—which I did after my first South Downs adventure—and its easy access through a tube coming just off my shoulder strap meant that I rehydrated early and often. All I needed to do to take a sip of water was to turn my head. On my second South Downs walk, I used a combination: a water reservoir to sip from as I walked, and a one-liter water bottle to take bigger drinks from when I stopped for a rest.

Some people complain about the water bladder making the water taste like plastic, but mine has no unusual taste whatsoever. Plus, it has a wide opening, and I can add a tray of ice cubes, keeping the water fresh for hours—this is especially nice on a hot summer day. I won't do another walk without my water reservoir.

The night before each day's walk, review your route for the following day and note the conditions: weather, temperature, water taps, facilities, etc. If rain is forecast, be sure your waterproofs are easily accessible. I keep mine at the bottom of my pack, which has a separate zippered opening. If it's going to be scorching hot and there are no water taps, plan to bring more water than you think you'll need.

Always bring more water than you think you'll need. I can't say this enough. It adds extra weight, but you don't want to risk your life to heatstroke or dehydration.

Lastly, are you a woman who might start her monthly cycle while on the walk? I did on my first walk, and while I spared you the details in this book, it was a bit challenging to take care of my monthly business at the side of the trail (my apologies if this is too much information for you). There was one moment where I thought I had found a bit of privacy, and then a car came down the trail next to me. I found it to be mildly frustrating, but not really a big deal. But if you can't imagine dealing with menstruation out in the wild, be sure to plan your walk during a different part of your cycle.

Plan in Advance

The first time around, I planned my trip two months in advance, but the people who seemed to get the best accommodation on the tricky nights had booked four or five months in advance. People plan early in England! Weekends are the most challenging time to get accommodation in the summer, so if you can't book that far in advance, try to not start your walk on the weekend. Start on a Monday instead, and walk until Friday and over the weekend and into the next week. That way, you only have two weekend days instead of three or four. That's what I did on my second South Downs journey. Plus, I booked all accommodation three months in advance, and I had no trouble getting the places I wanted to stay at.

Also, keep in mind that the points on the South Downs Way that are most busy are the two ends near Winchester and Eastbourne, and those are the stages where you'll see a lot of weekend walkers who will be requiring accommodation on those bits. Three villages were hard to find a place to stay on my first walk: the first night in Exton (which is why I ended up in nearby Droxford), Amberley (there was some kind of event going on), and Alfriston (I was staying there on a Friday night, and everything else was booked). Yet another reason to avoid departing or arriving on the weekend.

I live close enough to the South Downs Way that I could take a train early to Winchester and start my walk that same day and then take a train home from Eastbourne on my final day. But you might need an extra day's accommodation at the start and end of your journey, especially if you're coming from abroad. Take that into consideration with your planning.

Avoid Suffering

Suffering is optional, but if you really want to avoid it, you need to plan a bit more. Figure out what your pain points are by asking yourself what would make you the most miserable when walking, and plan ahead to avoid it. Think about sore muscles, aching feet, blisters, shoulder and back pain, headaches, sunburn, and heat. None of the above is pleasant, but most of these issues can be avoided if you plan well in advance. This section is not an exhaustive description of how to prevent each particular malaise and is just intended to be an introduction, so please do your own research online.

General soreness can be avoided by buying a great backpack, great boots or shoes (that fit you well, and that allow extra room for thick socks), and by packing light. This, of course, assumes that you're already in walking shape and that you're accustomed to heading up and down hills regularly. If not, you'll want to get in shape before you go. This takes time. If you don't have enough time to really get in shape and you still want to risk it, pack ibuprofen and a small tube of arnica cream to deal with the consequences. Arnica cream is my new lifesaver, but I've also heard great things about ibuprofen gel.

Blisters are generally caused by friction and can be avoided by:

- having good fitting boots or shoes (mine are a full size larger than my regular shoes) and the appropriate socks
- taking your socks off to air them and your feet out at breaks
- alternating between two pairs of socks each day, giving the second pair a chance to dry out before you swap them out again
- breaking your boots in for at least 100 miles before your main walk.

Be sure to read up online on all the ways to avoid blisters, as they can really make your walk miserable. If you do end up with blisters, be sure you've got alcohol to clean them off, a sewing kit with a needle you can drain the blisters with (I know you're not supposed to do this, but I do—drain at your own risk), and a collection of Compeed in different sizes to cover your blisters. Compeed is a lifesaver, though some people prefer moleskin, which I've never used.

Shoulder and back pain can be avoided with a lightweight pack that fits you well. I got lucky with my backpack (an Osprey Kyte 36), as it fits me so well it felt like it was part of my body. When picking it up to put it on, and when taking it off, I was aware that the pack was heavy, but when it was on my body, it felt like a perfect fit. The only issue I had was some chafing on my lower back on my first trip, but I solved that from the second day on by tying my long-sleeved base layer around my waist as extra padding. I didn't experience this same chafing on my second South Downs walk, probably because the weather wasn't as hot.

Headaches can be avoided by wearing a good sun hat (preferably one with a chin strap for wind) and by staying adequately hydrated. On my first South Downs walk, I wore my sun hat for about 95% of the time I was on the trail, with the only time I put it in my pack being during rain when I had my waterproof jacket and hood on. I'm particularly sensitive to the sun on my head, so I always keep covered when I'm out on a walk. The second time around, I wore a light buff as a wide headband, just to keep my head lightly covered. That worked just fine. Still, be sure to take your preferred headache remedy just in case.

Sunburn is an easy one: bring sunscreen at an appropriate strength for your skin. I had a small tube of SPF 50, and I still have some left. If you're wearing long pants, you'll just need to worry about your hands, arms, face, and neck. Remember that if you're using walking poles, your hands and lower arms will be more exposed to the sun than usual. I applied sunscreen at least twice daily to the backs of my hands, in addition to all the typical areas, and more frequently on the super hot days when I was sweating off all the sunscreen.

Train in Advance

If you've never done a long-distance walk before, you might want to do a trial walk of perhaps 2-3 days. If you're based in southeast England, the Downs Link trail is a good option for this: it's an old railway line that connects the North Downs Way with the South Downs Way and is quickly done over three days. My book, *Walking the Downs Link: Planning Guide & Reflections on Walking from St. Martha's Hill to Shoreham-by-Sea*, details my own walk. The Wey-South Path is another excellent option: this 36-mile (58 km) trail also connects the North Downs Way with the South Downs Way, starting in Guildford in the north and heading south to Amberley. I have another book about how to plan that journey: *Walking the Wey-South Path: Planning Guide & Reflections on Walking from Guildford to Amberley*.

You can also do a series of 2-3 day-walks back to back, based from your home. If you're based in Britain, Catherine Redfern has put together a series of weekend walks called Walk Your Weekend. You can purchase these detailed weekend guides from her website.

The critical detail on these walks is to load up your pack with the kind of weight you'll be bringing on a long-distance journey, to get used to walking with a heavier pack. Before setting out on the Way, I had thought I was an experienced hiker. But I had never walked with a heavy pack, and I had never done multiple day-walks in a row. The reality of this was sobering. Advanced training of this type will not only help you prepare physically for the walk, but it will give you the experience you need to acquire the mindset that you actually can complete a multi-day hike.

Travel Light

As a reminder: your pack should weigh no more than 10% of your body weight or a maximum of 17.6 pounds (8 kg.)...including water. The fact that I stretched the limits of the 10% rule for my backpack meant that my feet were always sore and blistered on my first South Downs walk.

Water is a Delicate Balance

Water is heavy, and it's a delicate balance between carrying too much (and thus hauling around too much weight) and not enough (and risking your life to dehydration, heat exhaustion, and heat stroke). Plan each day carefully, studying your guidebook or map the night before to see if there are any water taps or cafes along the way to fill up your water supply. This will mean you won't have to depart in the morning with your full water supply. However, there are some stretches of the Way that have no water taps or cafes at all. If you plan your itinerary as I did, you'll have to leave your B&B in the morning with all your water, which could be three-four quarts/liters, depending on the weather. Take hydration seriously.

PLANNING YOUR WALK

There are several things you'll need to take into consideration when planning your South Downs Way adventure: what time of the year is best, how much it will cost, and where you'll want to stay.

When to Walk

The weather in southeast England is relatively mild compared to other parts of the country, and if you're experienced in walking in cold weather, you might be open to exploring the South Downs Way at any time of the year. However, you'll probably find it most enjoyable between April and September. Summer in England is totally unpredictable, and the hot and sunny weather that I experienced during my walk would have been impossible to plan for (or to avoid).

If you want to avoid the possibility of such high heat (and thus the need to carry large quantities of water), you may prefer to book your walk in April or September, when it's less likely to be so warm. Early September, for me, was the perfect month for walking. England is not, of course, known for its sunny climate, so whether you choose to walk during summer or not, you'll want to carry a waterproof jacket and pants with you for protection from the rain. Walking for hours on end in wet clothing makes for a miserable experience, and it's worth the extra weight to carry the waterproofs. Statistically speaking, July and August should be the driest months. They are also the warmest months.

Budget

In 2015, I budgeted about £700 for the eight days. This broke down into seven nights of accommodation at £50 each night, and eight days of food at £30 per day, plus a single rail ticket from where I live in Surrey to Winchester, and then another single back from Eastbourne.

In total, I spent £400 on accommodation (but you could get this number down if you plan well in advance) and about £20-25 each day on food: a sandwich costs about £3, and dinner came in just under £20 each evening. Breakfast was always included with my accommodation, whether I was staying at a pub, a B&B, or an inn.

You might end up spending less. Or you could spend more if you enjoy having a pint or more of beer to relax after a long day's walk. I never had more than a half-pint with my dinner. The rail tickets cost £43 but would have been 30% less if I had remembered to bring my Network Railcard.

The total cost for my journey came in just under my original estimate, at roughly £643. This does not include gear I purchased specifically for this walk, such as my backpack, hiking boots, and items of clothing. These are things that I can re-use for day walks and future long-distance journeys.

I'd say this is a mid-range budget, and you could spend more or less depending on where you stay and where and what you choose to eat and drink. Inns will be less expensive than

B&Bs, and hostels and camping will cost even less. Most guidebooks will show you accommodation options in all price ranges.

Prices were a bit higher when I walked the trail in 2019, and I spent about £550 in accommodation alone—however, I did have an extra night's accommodation since I walked the trail in nine days instead of eight. I didn't, however, buy a packed lunch each day, because I realized I was fine with just breakfast and dinner. Dinner was still about £20 each evening.

Keep in mind that there are not many banks along the way, and most of the little villages where you'll probably be staying won't have one at all. If your B&B requests a deposit to book your room, ask to pay the full room rate rather than just the deposit. This will save you having to carry the cash to pay the balance, as many places don't take cards. Calculate your budget carefully and bring enough money to pay for everything. If you come across a spot or two that does accept cards, consider that an exception rather than a rule—however, I found that many more places took card payments in 2019 compared to 2015.

Where to Stay

After my first South Downs experience, I now—as a general rule—plan to stay within each village (rather than on the outskirts) to avoid extra walking to and from the B&B and to and from dinner in the evenings. When I've walked twelve to twenty miles during the day, I really don't want an extra walk added on at the end.

Also, remember that there are different ways to split up the Way into stages. You can walk it in seven, eight, nine, or more days. And even if you choose an eight-day walk as I did the first time, you may decide to split the stages up differently. Consult a guidebook and at least a couple of websites for different options. I found most of the places I stayed in the guide that I recommend in the Resources section below. When I walked this trail a second time, I planned for nine days rather than eight, so I could enjoy it more—and I did. It was nice to have a shorter day about halfway through.

Exton

The first time, I stayed two miles away in Droxford at the White Horse Inn and enjoyed the simple room and excellent service. If you book far enough in advance, you should be able to find availability in Exton village at the Manor House—which I thoroughly enjoyed on my second walk—or one mile away at the Corhampton Lane Farm, which is highly recommended in my guidebook. Meonstoke, a nearby village, is another option for accommodation. When you start booking your accommodation for your South Downs walk, be sure to start with Exton, which will be the trickiest place to find somewhere to stay.

Buriton

I stayed at Nursted Farm both times, which I absolutely loved, and I highly recommend it. The hosts were an absolute delight, and my room and bathroom were spacious and comfortable. The farm is, however, two miles off the Way, and it's in the middle of nowhere, so there aren't any options for dinner other than heading into Petersfield or Buriton. If you prefer accommodation in the village of Buriton, the Master Robert Inn is one option.

Cocking

Both times, I stayed at Moonlight Cottage, and I highly recommend them for both a comfortable, quiet room and a great breakfast and packed lunch. They have a gorgeous garden that's very comfortable to relax in after a long walk as it gets shady in the afternoon. They're very organized with breakfast orders and also with packed lunch orders, which was a delight. Now that the local pub has closed, and they're offering dinners, I really enjoyed the family-style dinner with other walkers.

Amberley

The first time, I stayed at Little Nailards, which is a private home that only opens up as a B&B when other accommodation is not available, but this was my absolute favorite place that I stayed along the Way in 2015. The house and garden were comfortable and beautiful, and my hosts were wonderful.

On my second journey, I stayed at The Sportsman, which was perfect for both accommodation and dinner. Be sure to ask for a room with a view on the backside of the property, so you can enjoy the Amberley Wildbrooks. The views are truly spectacular.

Bramber

Both times, I stayed at the Castle Inn Hotel: the first time in a spacious room and an en suite bathroom, the second time in a tiny room just big enough to fit the bed and a little table and chair (also with an en suite bathroom). The Castle Inn Hotel has its own restaurant, and there are a couple of others nearby. Bramber's sister village of Upper Beeding, which is equally close to the Way, seems to have more facilities in the village itself, including a large shop and a pharmacy, should you need it.

Pyecombe

There are a couple of options in this tiny little village. I stayed at Tallai House, which was lovely and comfortable with a delicious breakfast. However, the fact that they ask walkers not to wash clothes in the bathroom—and yet fail to offer another alternative—is quite frankly ridiculous for a B&B located on the South Downs Way. It clearly does not cater to walkers, and for that reason, I'd recommend booking elsewhere if you can. I heard good things about Kingsley House B&B, which is on the same street as Tallai House.

Lewes

I stayed at 1 Garden Cottages, which I really enjoyed, with an en suite bathroom and a spacious room. My host was accommodating with information regarding the local area, including recommending an excellent pub just steps from the B&B where I had a wonderful dinner. However, staying at this location added an extra mile walk to my journey, being all the way on the other side of town. And Lewes is not on the South Downs Way, but a couple of miles off the route, so I'd really recommend you avoid staying here—unless you want to take advantage of the shops and facilities that a large town has to offer. Some people will plan a rest day in Lewes before resuming the second half of their walk on the South Downs.

Kingston-near-Lewes

Learn from my mistake, and stay in Kingston, not Lewes. Nightingales B&B has the best mattresses I've ever slept on—I know this sounds ridiculous, but they were fantastic—and Jean, the host, is absolutely lovely, as is her assistant, Claude, the cat. It's just a short walk to the village pub for dinner, which has excellent Sunday roasts. Kingston is a charming, quiet place to stay not too far off the trail.

Alfriston

The first time, I stayed at <u>Riverdale House</u>, a ten-minute walk from the main village. I had a lovely room with a bathroom next to it, and an excellent breakfast. The hosts were very attentive. However, I highly recommend booking a B&B in the central part of the village, which has several historical options to choose from, including <u>The Star Inn</u>, which is said to date back to 1345, and is where I stayed when I walked the Eastbourne-Alfriston-Eastbourne loop.

The second time I walked the Way, I stayed at The George Inn, which is where I've always eaten dinner, and where I was upgraded to the spacious suite. It's definitely my favorite of all three places I stayed in Alfriston. It's a beautiful old property, and the food is fantastic. Plus, it's so lovely to stay in the main village.

PACKING LIST

I've split my list into items I used daily, things I used some days, and items I never used. I'm also providing commentary on what I plan to do differently on my next long-distance walk. Your packing list will be different depending on your needs, but many of the items will be similar.

I keep an updated list on my blog of all my favorite gear, along with links to purchase the items, in the blog post: Ultimate Gear and Packing List for Multi-Day Hikes and Walks.

www.hollyworton.com/multi

Items I Used Every Day

- **Alarm clock:** I brought one on my first trip, and I'm not quite sure why I did this, rather than using the alarm on my phone. The second time, I just used my silent alarm on my Fitbit. You could also use the alarm on your mobile phone rather than bringing a separate one.

- **Arnica cream:** I had used arnica before, in the form of homeopathic globules, but I'd never used the cream. My knees had been bothering me for a couple of weeks before I started the walk, and I was worried they'd get worse once I started hiking up and down hills. Two days before I left, I read online about arnica cream, went out and bought a small tube, and started using it. In less than 24 hours, no more knee pain. I applied it liberally to my legs and feet each evening on the Way, on every spot that ached. It was my wonder cream. It's also available in a gel form, and there are different brands.
- **Backpack:** Mine is an Osprey Kyte 36, and it was perfect in so many ways. It was just the right size, and it fit me perfectly. If you decide on an Osprey, you can browse their website and select a pack based on the level of importance of features such as: women's specific fit (if relevant to you), lightweight, torso adjustability, integrated rain cover, trampoline-mesh style back system to keep you cool, and the maximum number of entry points, pockets, and organization, among other things. I like the integrated rain cover on my Kyte, and it's got lots of entry points to store items, which is convenient.
- **Bags:** On my first journey, I brought a mesh bag for my second set of walking clothes, and another bag to keep my evening clothes together, along with all the things I used when I was at a B&B: toothbrush, Vaseline, etc. On my second trip, I put everything into separate dry bags, and that make it a lot more convenient to find things in the evenings when I arrived at my B&B. I had another canvas bag that I used for a purse when I was out in the evenings: I'd put my iPhone, iPad, reading glasses, and wallet in

there to go to the local pub for dinner. This I used on both trips.

- **Birkenstocks:** These saved my feet on Day 5 when my feet were hot, tired, and blistered from the previous day. I had debated long and hard whether to bring Birks or flip flops for my evening shoes, but these won out in the end. Mine are the Gizeh style, with the toe post (which, as you can imagine, gave me new blisters in new places that my boots hadn't). On my Downs Link walk, I left these at home and only brought a pair of flip flops, which were okay, except that they gave me new blisters when I wore them to walk around the village in the evening after dinner. On a future long-distance walk, I'd either bring these or hiking sandals if they were lightweight enough. One thing about Birks, they're both comfortable and super light. And the fact that they're open sandals means that your feet can air out. For my 2020 Camino Portugues walk, I've bought the Eva version of the Gizeh sandals, which are waterproof and can double as shower shoes— they might very well be the perfect blend of flip flop, shower shoe, and supportive sandal.
- **Boots:** My boots for my 2015 walk were Meindl Respond Lady Mid Gtx, which are Gore-Tex rather than leather. There's a whole debate online about whether you really need full hiking boots for a walk like this, and a lot of people believe that trail running shoes are actually better for the summer months, as they're lighter weight and also make it easier for your feet to breathe. My boots were very comfortable for single day walks, but they were like hot ovens on the South Downs. After this walk, I ended up getting a pair of lightweight Salomon X

ULTRA 2 GTX® W shoes, which combine trail running technology with a Gore-Tex hiking shoe. They're much cooler than my Meindls and have become my preferred shoe for long-distance summer walks—in fact, before they wore out, I bought a second pair because I loved them so much. These were the shoes I wore on my 2019 South Downs walk.

- **Clothes:** In 2015, I brought two sets of clothes: walking clothes and evening clothes. In the daytime, I wore my standard walking pants, which weren't really sports pants or hiking pants but dark green cotton. They were comfortable, and the fabric breathed well, and I loved them, but I really wished I had the zip-off convertible pants that other walkers had. They just give you more options, especially in the heat of the summer. Eventually, I upgraded to proper walking trousers, which is what I wore in 2019, and I bought zip-off pants in 2020, which I'm pleased with.

- For tops, I brought two short sleeve sports layers that were thin, cool, and easy to dry. They often dried overnight in my room. I brought two light sports bras (not the kind that is designed for lots of running or bouncing), three pairs of cotton underwear, and three pairs of socks. I was happy to have an extra pair of socks in case a pair didn't fully dry during the day, but I'd leave the third pair of panties at home next time. They were thin and almost always dried overnight. However, I do *not* recommend cotton undies for any kind of sporting activity where you'll be sweating. I'll spare you the details but go with something that's more moisture-wicking, especially if you'll be walking in the summer. Enough said.

- For evening wear, in 2015, I brought a light summer dress, regular bra, and a shrug for when it cooled down at night. I felt really comfortable in this, and it was great to be able to change out of my walking pants and top into something fresh and less restrictive, but I just couldn't justify the extra weight on my second trip. On my second walk, I just wore the next day's top and bra and the same pair of pants.

- **Clothes drying system:** I invented this myself, so there might be something better out there. However, everyone who saw it on my walk seemed to think it was a sound system for drying clothes while walking. It consists of three binder clips, which are attached to a key ring, which then hooks onto the backpack with a carabiner. I used one clip for each sock, and the third for my sports bra. Underwear usually dried overnight in my room, as did my top, though if either of these items failed to dry overnight, they were clipped to the outside of my pack as well.

- **Deodorant:** This is something that I brought in 2015, and that I've left at home on every subsequent walk. I had read online that there was no sense in bringing deodorant on a long-distance hike, and let's be honest: the only times I smelled fresh were in the evenings after showering and for the first hour or so of my walk. After that, no amount of deodorant would have kept me smelling good. It's a waste of space and weight. I have left the deodorant behind on my subsequent walks, and I have smelled no

worse without it than I did with it on the South
Downs.

- **Glasses:** On my first South Downs walk, I brought
  reading glasses for reading books on my iPad in the
  evenings, but did not bring sunglasses, as I don't
  usually use them. If I didn't use a specific
  prescription with different strength in each eye, I
  would buy the kind that folds up into a tiny box, as
  they'd take up less space and weight that way.
  Something to look for if you use reading glasses and
  have an easy prescription. On my second walk, I
  brought sunglasses, and I wore them once, for about
  an hour, before I removed them. I'm just not used to
  wearing them, and I found them annoying.
- **Guidebook:** I recommend a couple of guides in the
  Resources section, depending on which direction
  you choose to do the walk. Most people I came
  across on the Way also traveled with maps, but on
  my first walk, I opted to travel light and trust that the
  Way would be well signposted, which it was 98% of
  the time. The second time, I brought maps but didn't
  actually use them.
- **Lip balm:** Normally, I never use lip balm because I
  drink enough water to keep my skin hydrated. But if
  it's hot and sunny when you're walking the Way,
  you'll want to bring some. I used mine every single
  day, multiple times a day. Be sure it has sun
  protection in it.
- **Pedometer:** I brought one in 2015, but I left this at
  home the second time. I used to use it every time I
  went out on a day-walk, usually because I don't plan
  my walks and I like seeing how far I've come.
  However, the iPhone has a Health app that tracks
  your paces, distance, and how many flights of stairs

(or the equivalent) you've walked. Or, if you use a Fitbit, that will, of course, do the same for you—I love reviewing all the data from my walks, so I'm kind of addicted to mine.

- **Pills:** I used a small plastic baggie to bring my medication, vitamins, and supplements. I brought only enough for the time I'd be walking, and I brought only the things that were absolutely necessary, like magnesium, which really helps me with muscle recovery after exercise.
- **Poles:** I use Pacerpoles, which were designed by physiotherapist Heather Rhodes, based up in Windermere (Cumbria, in northern England). These are the best poles I've seen, and they're a conversation starter: they sparked a little chat with one couple on the Way because they were so thrilled with their Pacerpoles, too. Pacerpoles help to give you better posture when walking, better breathing, better stability (they've saved me from tripping and falling many times), and these poles, in particular, have the best handgrip of any poles I've seen. They're designed for a relaxed hand position with minimal grip, and they make getting up hills much, much more comfortable, which is great on such a hilly walk as the South Downs Way. I highly recommend them.
- **Sun hat:** This is also non-negotiable. I've got a good one from Columbia with a wide brim and a chin strap for the wind. Not super attractive, and one woman actually didn't recognize me when I waved to her at the end of the Way because I was no longer wearing it. But I'm sensitive to the sun on my head, and even if you think you aren't, you'll want to bring one. Or, if you're traveling in spring or fall, you could

wear a buff (one of those multi-functional neck tubes) and fold it up into a wide headband. That was sufficient for me in September, and I'm sensitive to the sun on my head.

- **Tech:** I brought my iPad in its case, which includes a small keyboard, and its charger. I had to bring a separate USB cable to charge the keyboard. I also brought my iPhone with its charger and USB cable. The iPad was easy to slide down the side of my backpack, and I stored all the cords and chargers in a little bag. I used the iPad for both writing up my daily experiences—which turned into the chapters of this book—and also for reading, as I had loaded several books onto it before I left. For future walks, I'll definitely bring it, as long as I'm staying in B&Bs and places where I can charge. I did, however, get an iPad mini after my first South Downs walk, which weighs much less and takes up less space. I also brought headphones to listen to music in the evenings. One thing I wasn't sure I'd use but did end up using daily on my first trip, was a digital voice recorder to make notes as I walked the trail. It made it easy to record my thoughts and observations as I walked and add those details to this book. However, in the future, I'd just use the voice recording app on my phone.
- **Tissues:** Handy, as my hay fever was driving me crazy for the first three days. I ended up using the entire pack I brought and then buying another in Cocking. Or, bring a cloth handkerchief and wash it out in the evenings. They usually dry quickly.
- **Toiletries:** I kept these to a minimum: sunscreen in a small tube, travel-sized toothpaste, and toothbrush, hand sanitizer for cleaning off and

draining blisters. This is all stuff I'd bring again. Most hotels had liquid or bar soap and shampoo, but if you're staying at hostels, you'll need your own.

- **Travel hairbrush:** I found a small, lightweight one by Denman, the kind that folds open and has a mirror on one side, and you pop out the plastic bristles on the other side. This was lightweight and good to have on my first trip, but I didn't bring it on my second journey. I just "combed" my hair with my fingers, and that was good enough.

- **Wallet:** Just before I was getting ready to leave, I transferred the essentials to a much smaller wallet: a bit of cash and three cards. I did, however, forget my Network Railcard, which gets me a discount on train travel in the Southeast, and also my National Trust card, so be sure to double-check everything if you're downsizing your wallet for the trip.

- **Water:** On my first journey, I brought a 750 ml. stainless steel bottle, and used between two and four additional 500 ml. plastic bottles to supplement, depending on the weather and the availability of water taps along the way. If you opt for bottles rather than a bladder, leave the stainless steel bottle at home. Compared to plastic bottles, stainless steel is ridiculously heavy. As I mentioned, I purchased a water reservoir for my Downs Link walk, the Osprey Hydraulics™ LT 2.5L Reservoir, which I love. I've heard the water doesn't always taste that great in a bladder, so it depends on the brand, but it makes it easy to carry water on your back, and you've got easy access to it via a tube that comes over your shoulder and clips to your backpack strap. I know that I'm now better hydrated when I hike with my water reservoir *and* a lightweight, reusable plastic water bottle.

Items I Used Some Days

- **Compeed:** I will always bring Compeed on a walk like this, even if I someday learn the Super Secret to Blister Prevention (if there is such a secret). I think I've already sung the praises of Compeed, so I won't say anything else. It's not cheap, but it's worth every penny. Get more of this stuff than you think you'll need.

- **Knife:** I can't even remember at this point what I used my Swiss army knife for, but I didn't use it more than once or twice. I didn't bring it on my second walk.

- **Long-sleeved base layer:** On Day 1, I thought this was a total waste, and I regretted having brought it. However, I used it on Days 2-8 to alleviate the chafing from my backpack on my lower back by tying it around my waist. It worked like magic. In 2019, I didn't bring one, and I didn't miss it at all.

- **Pen:** I brought a ballpoint pen to make notes, but rarely used it. Still, I'd probably bring one again. It's small and lightweight, and it doesn't hurt to have one. I also like to have a highlighter to mark up things in my guidebook.

- **Snacks:** On my first trip, I brought too many snacks: a bag each of almonds, cashews, dried bananas, and figs. In the end, I ate the whole bag of dried bananas and just a few cashews. In the future, I'll just bring one thing: dried bananas, which are lightweight. I didn't snack anywhere near as much as I thought I would, with breakfasts being so filling. On my second trip, I brought one small bag of nuts, and a small bar of chocolate, and that was fine for the whole week.

- **Tampons:** Yep, I managed to plan a 100-mile walk through the middle of nowhere and my cycle started on Day 6. I knew this before I left, so I was prepared with a little baggie of tampons. If the same thing happens to you, be sure to bring a couple of extra plastic baggies to store used tampons in after you've changed them behind a bush along the trail (assuming you're lucky enough to find a bush to use). And (if you're a woman), please, please, please do check your cycle before you leave, so you know if you'll be expecting your period halfway through your journey. You want to be prepared for this, either with tampons or a Mooncup or cloth pads...or whatever it is that you use.

- **Travel sewing kit:** This was essential in my blister care: I used the pins in the sewing kit to drain blisters. Yes, yes, I know you're not supposed to do this, but I do. My travel sewing kit is small and lightweight.

- **Vaseline:** A lot of backpacking blogs recommend covering your feet with a thin layer of Vaseline to ward off blisters. This had been recommended by a friend, and so I tried this technique for the first four days...until I got blisters, did some more research, and found out that other people recommend keeping your foot skin as dry as possible, so I gave up after that. If you decide to try this method, get one of those small tins of Vaseline that are supposed to be for your lips, which is what I used. It had more than enough Vaseline for the week. All the same, I didn't use Vaseline on my feet ever again.

- **Waterproofs:** I have a North Face waterproof jacket and Berghaus waterproof pants. I only wore them one day, when it rained for a couple of hours on Day 6 in 2015, and once on my second journey. However, these are non-negotiable for me: I never go on a walk without them.

Items I Never Used

- **Asthma inhaler:** My asthma is generally brought on by allergies such as hay fever, so I always make sure to have an inhaler with me if I'm going on a walk. I got a new one before I left as the previous one had expired, and I'd definitely bring one with me again. The middle of nowhere is no place to have an asthma attack without an inhaler. This should go without saying: bring any and all medication that you need.

- **Business cards:** What on earth was I thinking bringing business cards? I know what I was thinking: that I'd be socializing and making life-long friends on the Way, and we'd want to stay in touch afterward. Well, out of all the people I met, I only know the first names of one couple, who I met at the farm on my second night. Everyone else I crossed paths with, I didn't even get their name. I haven't kept in touch with anyone I met on the South Downs, and it's not for lack of business cards. These will stay at home next time...obviously. I hope you're having a good laugh right now at my silliness. Don't bring business cards!

- **Compass:** Didn't use it once, but this is one of those necessary things I always have with me on a walk. While most mobile phones have a compass app, they often don't work well in remote areas, which is when you need it most. Despite excellent signage on the South Downs Way, I will always bring a compass.
- **Earplugs:** I added these at the last minute, and despite the raging party at the inn on my first night in Droxford in 2015, I wouldn't bring these again. I was so tired every night that I didn't have trouble sleeping, and I didn't even bother digging out the earplugs for that first night. But you might be extra sensitive to noise, so evaluate what's best for you.
- **First aid kit:** On both trips, I brought a very compact one I found online, and never used it, but this is another one of those things that you've really got to have around, just in case.
- **Flashlight:** I never used this, and most of the B&Bs I stayed at had a flashlight in the room for emergency use. I walked during BST, so there was no risk of being out on the trail after dark (except on that super long twenty-mile day when I thought I'd arrive just before sunset). It's tempting to not bring one, but it's good practice to have one, so I always carry one in my pack.
- **House keys:** This seemed like unnecessary weight because Agustin walked me to and from the rail station when I left and arrived, but I wanted to be sure I could get back in the house in case his plans changed for my return, and he couldn't be there.
- **Titanium spork:** This may seem odd, but I always used to carry one of these in my handbag. If I'm eating on the go, it means I can pick up a salad

instead of having to eat a sandwich. Super convenient at many times, but I didn't use it once on the South Downs Way, and I didn't bring it again. Salads do not pack well, and thus I ended up eating a sandwich for lunch every day.

- **Whistle:** Never used it, but it's so small I'll definitely keep it on my backpack. It's an essential safety device that's easy enough to carry around. Do you know the signal for distress? It's six good long blasts. Stop for one minute. Repeat. Continue in this manner until someone reaches you, and don't stop just because you've heard a reply – your rescuers may be using your whistle blasts as a way to figure out exactly where you are.

THE COUNTRYSIDE CODE OF 2014

R espect. Protect. Enjoy. In 2004, the UK Countryside Code replaced the Country Code, which dates back to the 1930s. This document details responsibilities for visitors to the countryside and for those who manage the land. The section that concerns walkers is divided into three main areas: respect other people, protect the natural environment, and enjoy the outdoors. Much of it is common sense for anyone who has grown up in rural areas, but for those who haven't, it's worth reading through, which is why I'm including it in this book. The entire document can be found online, including the section that concerns landowners in rural areas. Reprinted below with permission via the Open Government Licence is the most recent version at time of this publication, dating back to 23 October 2014.

Respect other people

Please respect the local community and other people using the outdoors. Remember your actions can affect people's lives and livelihoods.

Consider the local community and other people enjoying the outdoors

Respect the needs of local people and visitors alike – for example, don't block gateways, driveways or other paths with your vehicle.

When riding a bike or driving a vehicle, slow down or stop for horses, walkers and farm animals and give them plenty of room. By law, cyclists must give way to walkers and horse-riders on bridleways.

Co-operate with people at work in the countryside. For example, keep out of the way when farm animals are being gathered or moved and follow directions from the farmer.

Busy traffic on small country roads can be unpleasant and dangerous to local people, visitors and wildlife - so slow down and where possible, leave your vehicle at home, consider sharing lifts and use alternatives such as public transport or cycling. For public transport information, phone Traveline on 0871 200 22 33 or visit www.traveline.org.uk.

Leave gates and property as you find them and follow paths unless wider access is available

A farmer will normally close gates to keep farm animals in, but may sometimes leave them open so the animals can reach food and water. Leave gates as you find them or follow instructions on signs. When in a group, make sure the last person knows how to leave the gates.

Follow paths unless wider access is available, such as on open country or registered common land (known as 'open access land').

If you think a sign is illegal or misleading such as a 'Private - No Entry' sign on a public path, contact the local authority.

Leave machinery and farm animals alone – don't interfere

with animals even if you think they're in distress. Try to alert the farmer instead.

Use gates, stiles or gaps in field boundaries if you can – climbing over walls, hedges and fences can damage them and increase the risk of farm animals escaping.

Our heritage matters to all of us – be careful not to disturb ruins and historic sites.

Protect the natural environment

We all have a responsibility to protect the countryside now and for future generations, so make sure you don't harm animals, birds, plants or trees and try to leave no trace of your visit. When out with your dog make sure it is not a danger or nuisance to farm animals, horses, wildlife or other people.

Leave no trace of your visit and take your litter home

Protecting the natural environment means taking special care not to damage, destroy or remove features such as rocks, plants and trees. They provide homes and food for wildlife, and add to everybody's enjoyment of the countryside.

Litter and leftover food doesn't just spoil the beauty of the countryside, it can be dangerous to wildlife and farm animals – so take your litter home with you. Dropping litter and dumping rubbish are criminal offences.

Fires can be as devastating to wildlife and habitats as they are to people and property – so be careful with naked flames and cigarettes at any time of the year. Sometimes, controlled fires are used to manage vegetation, particularly on heaths and moors between 1 October and 15 April, but if a fire appears to be unattended then report it by calling 999.

Keep dogs under effective control

When you take your dog into the outdoors, always ensure it does not disturb wildlife, farm animals, horses or other people by keeping it under effective control. This means that you:

- keep your dog on a lead, or
- keep it in sight at all times, be aware of what it's doing and be confident it will return to you promptly on command
- ensure it does not stray off the path or area where you have a right of access
- Special dog rules may apply in particular situations, so always look out for local signs – for example:
- dogs may be banned from certain areas that people use, or there may be restrictions, byelaws or control orders limiting where they can go
- the access rights that normally apply to open country and registered common land (known as 'open access' land) require dogs to be kept on a short lead between 1 March and 31 July, to help protect ground nesting birds, and all year round near farm animals
- at the coast, there may also be some local restrictions to require dogs to be kept on a short lead during the bird breeding season, and to prevent disturbance to flocks of resting and feeding birds during other times of year
- it's always good practice (and a legal requirement on 'open access' land) to keep your dog on a lead around farm animals and horses, for your own safety and for the welfare of the animals. A farmer may shoot a dog which is attacking or chasing farm

animals without being liable to compensate the
dog's owner
- however, if cattle or horses chase you and your dog,
it is safer to let your dog off the lead – don't risk
getting hurt by trying to protect it. Your dog will be
much safer if you let it run away from a farm animal
in these circumstances and so will you
- everyone knows how unpleasant dog mess is and it
can cause infections, so always clean up after your
dog and get rid of the mess responsibly –' bag it and
bin it'. Make sure your dog is wormed regularly to
protect it, other animals and people

Enjoy the outdoors

Even when going out locally, it's best to get the latest information about where and when you can go. For example, your
rights to go onto some areas of open access land and coastal
land may be restricted in particular places at particular times.
Find out as much as you can about where you are going, plan
ahead and follow advice and local signs.

Plan ahead and be prepared

You'll get more from your visit if you refer to up-to-date maps
or guidebooks and websites before you go. Visit Natural
England on GOV.UK or contact local information centres or
libraries for a list of outdoor recreation groups offering advice
on specialist activities.

You're responsible for your own safety and for others in
your care – especially children - so be prepared for natural
hazards, changes in weather and other events. Wild animals,
farm animals and horses can behave unpredictably if you get

too close, especially if they're with their young - so give them plenty of space.

Check weather forecasts before you leave. Conditions can change rapidly especially on mountains and along the coast, so don't be afraid to turn back. When visiting the coast check for tide times at easytide.ukho.gov.uk, don't risk getting cut off by rising tides and take care on slippery rocks and sea-weed.

Part of the appeal of the countryside is that you can get away from it all. You may not see anyone for hours, and there are many places without clear mobile phone signals, so let someone else know where you're going and when you expect to return.

Follow advice and local signs

England has about 190,000 km (118,000 miles) of public rights of way, providing many opportunities to enjoy the natural environment. Get to know the signs and symbols used in the countryside to show paths and open countryside. See the Countryside Code leaflet for more detail.

RESOURCES

Here are some resources that can help you plan your South Downs Way journey. I recommend getting a good guidebook, such as the one I used, which is now in its sixth edition.

Guidebooks & Maps

South Downs Way: Trailblazer British Walking Guide, by Jim Manthorpe

This is an excellent guidebook for walking from Winchester to Eastbourne. There are 60 large-scale maps in the book, including guides to 49 villages along the Way. Most of the maps are handwritten, and include a wealth of practical information, such as where water taps are located along the way. This information is invaluable when planning each stage. Before departing on my journey, I took a handful of highlighters and colored in different bits on each map: I highlighted the trail in yellow, water taps in blue, warnings in pink (things like "don't miss this turn"), natural points of interest in green (Chancton-bury Ring, for example) and other details in orange (such as the visitor centre and cafe in the Queen Elizabeth Country Park). This guidebook also includes lists of itineraries of different lengths, depending on whether you want to stay at B&Bs or whether you'll be camping and staying in hostels. Its fourth edition is from 2012, so it's still pretty accurate, though there is a fifth edition from June 2015 that I just missed before I headed out on my walk.

South Downs Way National Trails Guide, by Paul Millmore

This is the guidebook to get if you're walking the other direction, from Eastbourne to Winchester, and it's the official National Trail guide. Not having used it, I can't say more, but if you're planning your journey from east to west, this is the book you'll need.

South Downs Way AZ Adventure Series (Adventure Atlas)

A couple of the people I crossed paths with on the Way had this map book, and they were all very happy with it. It contains the full Ordnance Survey maps in a convenient book format. The maps were very useful at the few points where the trail wasn't very well signposted, and I have since purchased this map to have on hand for my next South Downs walk.

London Hiker

http://londonhiker.com

Catherine Redfern runs the London Hiker website, and has created two fantastic online resources to help you plan a long distance walk: Trail Walking for First Timers, a three week e-course, and Walk Your Weekends, a multimedia guide to Catherine's top 14 weekend walking getaways in Britain. If you live in the UK and are interested in Walk Your Weekends, you'll want to purchase that, as Trail Walking for First Timers is included in WYW. Both are affordably priced, at £19.99 and £47.

National Trails Website

http://www.nationaltrail.co.uk/

This is the official website for the fifteen National Trails of England and Wales and has trail information, trail news, and tips on planning your walk. You can also request a certificate of completion after you walk the South Downs Way.

Rambling Man

http://ramblingman.org.uk/walks/southdownsway/

This is a blog written by Andrew Bowden, who chronicles an eight-day walk of the South Downs Way, split into various weekends. He is also, coincidentally, Catherine Redfern's (of London Hiker) other half. I read both their blogs for years, and only recently realized the connection. I digress. Andrew's blog is what helped me to originally decide to walk the South Downs Way rather than the North Downs Way, which is closer to home. His perspective is also good if you're thinking of walking the Way in weekends rather than all at once, as I did.

South Downs Discovery

http://www.southdownsdiscovery.com/

This is a travel agency that specializes in self-guided walking holidays and baggage transfers along the South Downs Way. I'm including them here because they have an excellent description of different itineraries along the Way that range from six days to nine days, with two options for seven day walks and another two for an eight day walk. These can help give you an idea of how you want to split up each stage of the walk. It's a good idea to evaluate all the different options.

Akashic Records

Vickie Young is my contact for all things Akashic Records. She's the one who sends the weekly emails from my Records Keepers. She also offers one-to-one sessions to access your own Records.

https://www.medicinedreamhealing.com/

Oracle cards

The deck of cards that I used for my first South Downs adventure was Lisa McLoughlin's Plant Ally Deck.

https://www.lisamcloughlinart.com/

The cards I used on my second South Downs walk was the Spiritsong Tarot deck. You can find them wherever you purchase books online, or get them directly from the publisher.

http://www.usgamesinc.com

Blog Posts

I've written a series of blog posts that you might find useful in preparing your future outdoor adventures. You can find for them on my blog at:

http://www.hollyworton.com/blog

Ultimate Gear and Packing List for Backpacking and Car Camping: www.hollyworton.com/camping

Ultimate Gear and Packing List for Multi-Day Hikes and Walks: www.hollyworton.com/multi

Ultimate Gear and Packing List for One-Day Hikes and Walks: www.hollyworton.com/daywalk

On the Podcast

I've also got a series of podcast episodes on Nature and my outdoors adventures. You can find them here:

www.hollyworton.com/podcast

ON THE PODCAST

The Into the Woods podcast is about personal growth through outdoor adventures.

You can find Holly's show on Apple Podcasts, or wherever you listen to podcasts. Links to subscribe, as well as the full list of episodes, can be found here:

http://www.hollyworton.com/podcast/

The following episodes may be of interest to you. Most of the episodes below have downloadable transcripts (no email required to get the pdf)—or you can read the transcript online in the show notes.

- 390 Holly Worton ~ What to Do When You Don't Feel Like Having Adventures
- 386 Heather Waring ~ Walking for Personal Development and Self Care
- 383 Anne Malambo ~ How Solo Travel Can Change Our Lives
- 382 Holly Worton ~ Know Your Why For Your Outdoor Adventures

- 381 Helen Forester ~ How Getting Outdoors Can Help Us Release Creative Blocks
- 378 Holly Worton ~ How to Balance Your Hobbies When You're a Multipassionate Person
- 377 Holly Worton ~ How to Prioritize Your Hobbies and Adventures
- 376 Holly Worton ~ Long Distance Walks: Time and Space to Think and Reflect
- 375 Joanna Hennon + Holly ~ How Oracle Cards Can Enrich Your Outdoor Adventures
- 374 Holly Worton ~ How Outdoors Adventures + Travel Help With Digital Detox
- 373 How Outdoors Adventures Can Help You Give Yourself Permission to Be You
- 372 Holly Worton ~ How Outdoors Adventures Can Help Us Achieve Our Life Goals
- 370 Brad Borkan ~ How Outdoors Adventures Can Help You Make Better Decisions In Life
- 369 Holly Worton ~ Getting Out of Your Comfort Zone With Outdoor Adventures
- 368 Yvette Webster ~ How to Take Your Hiking to the Next Level
- 367 Holly Worton ~ Finding Yourself Through Solo Travel and Outdoor Adventures
- 364 Holly Worton – Personal Growth Through Outdoor Adventure
- 359 Adam Wells ~ How To Prepare For Your First Long Distance Trail
- 354 Stephen Marriott ~ The Life-changing Magic of Walking a Long-Distance Trail

ABOUT THE AUTHOR

Holly Worton is a podcaster and author. Her 2019 book, *If Trees Could Talk: Life Lessons from the Wisdom of the Woods*, went straight to the top of 16 Amazon bestseller lists, and she has been featured on BBC Radio Scotland and on prime time national television in the UK—on ITV's This Morning and Channel 4's show Steph's Packed Lunch.

She helps people get to know themselves better through connecting with Nature, so they can feel happier and more fulfilled. Holly enjoys spending time outdoors. She loves trail running, walking long-distance trails and exploring Britain's sacred sites. She's originally from California and now lives in England's Surrey Hills, but she has also lived in Spain, Costa Rica, Mexico, Chile, and Argentina. Holly is a member of the Druid order OBOD.

Podcast

You can find her podcast on Apple Podcasts, or wherever you listen to podcasts. Links to subscribe, as well as the full list of episodes, can be found here:
  http://www.hollyworton.com/podcast/

Patreon

You can support her work and get access to her ebooks by joining her on Patreon:
  https://www.patreon.com/hollyworton

Books

You can find her other work—including her books on business mindset, nature, and walking long-distance trails—wherever you purchased this title.

Newsletter

Finally, you can stay in touch by subscribing to her newsletter on her main website:
  http://www.hollyworton.com/

Social media

ALSO BY HOLLY WORTON

Nature books

- *If Trees Could Talk: Life Lessons from the Wisdom of the Woods*
- *If Trees Could Talk: Life Lessons from the Wisdom of the Woods — A Companion Workbook*

Walking books

- *Alone on the South Downs Way: A Tale of Two Journeys from Winchester to Eastbourne*
- *Walking the Downs Link: Planning Guide & Reflections on Walking from St. Martha's Hill to Shoreham-by-Sea*
- *Alone on the Ridgeway: A Tale of Two Journeys Between Avebury and Ivinghoe Beacon*
- *Walking the Wey-South Path: Planning Guide & Reflections on Walking from Guildford to Amberley*

Personal growth

- *The Year You Want*

Into the Woods Short Reads

- *How to Add More Adventure to Your Life*
- *How to Practice Self-Love: Actual Steps You Can Take To Love Yourself More*

- *How to Practice Self Care: Even When You Think You're Too Busy*
- *How to Develop Your Own Inner Compass: Learn to Trust Yourself and Easily Make the Best Decisions*
- *Into the Woods Short Reads: Box Set Books 1-5*

Business Mindset series

- *Business Beliefs: Upgrade Your Mindset to Overcome Self Sabotage, Achieve Your Goals, and Transform Your Business (and Life)*
- *Business Beliefs: A Companion Workbook*
- *Business Blocks: Transform Your Self-Sabotaging Mind Gremlins, Awaken Your Inner Mentor, and Allow Your Business Brilliance to Shine*
- *Business Blocks: A Companion Workbook*
- *Business Visibility: Mindset Shifts to Help You Stop Playing Small, Dimming Your Light and Devaluing Your Magic*
- *Business Visibility: A Companion Workbook*
- *Business Intuition: Tools to Help You Trust Your Own Instincts, Connect with Your Inner Compass, and Easily Make the Right Decisions*
- *Business Intuition: A Companion Workbook*
- *Business Mindset Books: Box Set Books 1-4*

En español

- *Si los árboles hablaran: enseñanzas de vida desde la sabiduría de los árboles*
- *El año que quieres: imagina la vida que deseas y planea tu año ideal, para no dejarlos al azar*

REVIEW TEAM

Would you like to be a part of my review team?

I really value the feedback and reviews I get from my readers. They make a huge difference in helping me (and other authors) reach new people. I know that it takes time to read and review a book, and I value the time people put into this. Thank you so much!

Here's what's involved....

Advance Review Copies

Whenever I have a new book coming out, I will send you an email to see if you would like to get an advance ebook copy for review on Amazon and/or Goodreads (or elsewhere online!).

If you are able to write an honest review by the deadline (I'll let you know about the timeline), then I'll send over a copy for you to read before it's on sale to the general public.

I can also send you free copies of any of my existing books (ebooks or audio) if you'd like to review them.

Audiobooks

If you enjoy audiobooks, I can also provide free audiobook codes so you can listen to the new audiobooks and review online. I don't produce all of my books as audiobooks, but I will offer you codes for the ones that are available.

Your review

If you enjoy the book, please post your review on Amazon.com or your local Amazon.

You can also post reviews on the online bookstores, social media, your blog, and anywhere else you feel like sharing. Amazon is the biggie for online reviews, but Goodreads, Instagram, and other online outlets all help.

Unsubscribe

This is a simple email list, so if you change your mind about being involved for whatever reason, you can unsubscribe from the list at any time.

Join now

If you would like to join, please fill out the form on my website and then look out for an email confirmation. Learn more here: https://www.hollyworton.com/review-team/.

HOLLY'S GROVE

I'd love for you to join me in my private community for readers, Patrons, clients, and students only. It's a place to talk about tree communication and outdoors adventures. You can ask any questions if you have them.

I'll also be sharing updates about my upcoming book projects and launches.

This is a general group, so we'll be talking both trees and outdoors adventures - and basically all the stuff I write about.

I'd love to get to know you in there!

You can find it here:
http://hollyworton.com/grove

A REQUEST

If you enjoyed this book, please review it online. It takes just a couple of minutes to write a quick review. It would mean the world to me! Good reviews help other readers to discover new books.

Thank you, thank you, thank you.

Printed in Great Britain
by Amazon

84258529R00174